P9-DVV-336

1001 Things Every College Student Needs to Know
Copyright © 2008 by Harry H. Harrison Jr.

Published in Nashville, Tennessee, by Thomas Nelson. Thomas Nelson
is a registered trademark of HarperCollins Christian Publishing, Inc.

Project Editor: Lisa Stilwell

Designed by ThinkPen Design, LLC

ISBN-10: 1–4041–0434–8
ISBN-13: 978–1–4041–0434–1

Printed and bound in the United States of America

www.thomasnelson.com

1001 Things
Every College
Student Needs
to Know

(Like Buying Your Books Before Exams Start)

HARRY H. HARRISON JR.

THOMAS NELSON
Since 1798

NASHVILLE   MEXICO CITY   RIO DE JANEIRO

Table of Contents

Introduction

Before you step foot on campus, we need to have a talk.

More kids than ever are applying to college because they know that in this computerized, global economy, a bachelor's degree holds the keys to the kingdom—but more students than ever are leaving school without a degree. In fact, one in three Americans in their midtwenties are college dropouts. Only 54 percent of college freshmen graduate within six years.

Let's not dwell on how your parents have destroyed their 401(k)s to send you to school. Or how you've taken out student loans that you can only hope to pay back if you have a medical degree. Let's focus on what's actually happening here. Students are showing up on campus unprepared for the course load, ill equipped to prioritize, helpless to solve problems without Mom running interference, and lacking the inner strength to stand up to the pressures, demands, and challenges they will inevitably face the next four years. Or more.

If that's you, don't flee to a community college—the statistics there are really grim. While there are exceptions, most community-college students never make it to a four-year school. Besides, this is not the time to set your sights low. Kids with just one or two years of college are paid little better than high-school graduates.

The fact is, you need to know a few things. Well, maybe about a thousand things. Because college grades, graduate school, and test scores determine who will carry an American Express Platinum Card in the future. If you graduate from any four-year school, the system is on your side. But the system is definitely against you if you do something brainless.

Like leave college. This is a world where the educated get richer and the uneducated get poorer.

So the message here is simple. Don't let something stupid like too much partying, a bad romance, not buying books on time, or chronic disorganization ruin the rest of your life. You need staying power. This book is how to get it. •

You Need to Know How to Prepare for College

1. You need to know you'll have to beat the odds. According to American College Testing (ACT), one in every four college students leaves before completing their sophomore year. And nearly half of all freshmen will either drop out before obtaining a degree, or they'll leave to complete their degree elsewhere.

•

2. You need to know your ticket to the upper middle-class is punched with a college degree.

•

3. You need to know this is the time to shoot for excellence.

4. You need to know you're not entitled to a college degree. In fact, you're no longer entitled to anything.

5. You need to know how to read really, really fast. If you don't, take a speed-reading course.

•

6. You need to know what it takes to be prepared. The top schools are looking for:

- Four years of English or a 21 on the ACT English section (530 SAT verbal)

- Four years of math (Algebra I, Geometry, Algebra II, and an advanced math class for which Algebra II is a prerequisite) or a 24 ACT/540 SAT

- One year each of biology, chemistry, or physics or a 20 on the ACT Science

- Three years of social studies

- Three years of the same foreign language

- One year of a fine art

- Ranking in the top quarter of your high-school class or ACT of 22 or SAT of 2200 or a 3.0 GPA (4.0=A)

7. You need to know it's important to accomplish something during your senior year of high school. Kids who coast that last year aren't mentally or emotionally prepared for the workload college will dump on them.

8. You need to know over one-third of the people who drop out of college do so because they can't handle the workload.

•

9. You need to know homework, responsibility, and self-discipline take on different meanings in college.

•

10. You need to know that if you avoid taking hard classes in high school, you'll lower your odds of graduating from college.

•

11. You need to know that everything you thought in high school—about studying, hard work, achievement, meeting people, how cool you were—is all out the window.

12. You need to know what you're signing up for: constant studying, difficult exams, pressure to perform, organizing your time, prioritizing your work, meeting expectations, and acting like an adult. And some unforgettable parties.

•

13. You need to know it doesn't matter who you were in high school. Nobody cares. But it does matter who you think you are now.

•

14. You need to know to forget what Mister Rogers told you years ago: You're not special. In fact, there's room for improvement.

15. You need to know how to
do your homework without your
mother threatening you.

16. You need to know how
to have an original thought.
This ability really helps.

17. You need to know the more
college-prep classes you take, the more
prepared for college you'll actually be.

18. You need to know that
if you work your butt off in
high school while everybody else
is out partying, colleges will
pay you to come to their school.

19. You need to know this is when all those AP classes you took pay off. You could actually "place out" of most of your freshman year, saving you time and up to $25,000.

•

20. You need to know enough logic to be able to interpret tables and graphs. If you don't, take remedial logic classes now.

•

21. You need to know how to read an editorial and comprehend what position the author is taking. If you're mystified about what's going on, you need to take remedial reading classes.

22. You need to know that if you've acquired the discipline to keep studying even when you're tired and bored, you can graduate from Harvard early.

•

23. You need to know to not spend the summer before your freshman year wasted. The smart students already know the first-semester's reading assignments and are getting ahead.

•

24. You need to know how to practice analytical thinking. Be able to define problems, collect facts, form a hypothesis, conduct an analysis, and develop a solution. (If you don't know the meaning of these words, head to a community college.)

25. You need to know how to brainstorm on your own. The good students aren't always eager to share their ideas.

•

26. You need to know college is a rough place to learn you're not the center of the universe.

•

27. You need to know to be reading something denser than text messages.

•

28. You need to know college (like the real world afterward) is all about creative solutions. Those are found in your head.

•

29. You need to know how to defend your opinions and values. They will be challenged regularly.

30. You need to know you won't get as much praise as you got in high school. College professors don't really care about your feelings or that you "worked hard" all weekend.

•

31. You need to know if you're unable to do fundamental computation, you don't need to be taking college math. You need to be taking remedial math. Or acting classes.

•

32. You need to know to not choose a college because it was featured on MTV.

•

33. You need to know to judge a college based on things like degrees offered, class sizes, proximity to home, campus life, cost, cost, and cost. These things can all be graduation wreckers.

34. You need to know, when visiting schools, not to be swayed by new dorm rooms and a cool new workout center. This is called "marketing." Ask to see the library. Maybe a science classroom.

•

35. You need to know to take advantage of campus visitation opportunities before you select a college. Sit in on a class, walk the campus, talk to students, and go to a party or two.

•

36. You need to know how far away you want to live from Mom and Dad and your boyfriend. Loneliness is a big reason kids flame out.

37. You need to know if a college
costs $40,000 a year and you have
limited resources, you'll spend more time
worrying about money than studying.

●

38. You need to know if
endless days of overcast, rainy skies
make you want to shoot yourself,
there are campuses to avoid.

●

39. You need to know
going to a school that's either
too large or too small can result
in the same thing—leaving.

40. You need to know if your family doesn't have money, you've got it that much harder. Three-quarters of the students at top colleges come from the top socioeconomic quarter, with only 10 percent from the poorer half and 3 percent from the bottom quarter (2004 study by the Century Foundation, a policy institute in New York).

•

41. You need to know whether you're ready. There's a lot to be said for taking a year off to work for the Peace Corps or with Doctors Without Borders or even to travel Europe. Do something to stimulate your thought process.

42. You need to know
taking a year off before you start
school won't impact your college
admission. In fact, many top-
tier schools think it's a great idea.

•

43. You need to know
how to express yourself
professionally before you enroll.

•

44. You need to know college
is work. Some fun. Lots of work.
As much work as your parents
are putting in to raise the funds.

45. You need to know that until you demonstrate an ability to handle basic algebra, most colleges won't allow you to take courses in many majors.

•

46. You need to know instant messaging and term papers are two entirely different forms of writing.

•

47. You need to know how to write a good sentence. And realize there could be a student from China next to you who can probably write a better one than you.

48. You need to know you
can achieve what you desire.
If graduating from college is
the most important thing in the
world to you, you'll graduate. Period.
If partying is the most important
thing to you, you'll have great fun.
You won't graduate, but you'll have fun.

•

49. You need to know that you can
meet members of your freshman class
on Facebook and Twitter months
before you head to campus. Someone,
somewhere, has set up a group for your class.

50. You need to know that
on Facebook you can discuss
roommate issues, dorm issues,
boy issues, and even arrange to meet
each other before school starts.

•

51. You need to know that preparation
is a key to graduation. Showing up to
class unprepared means a quick turn in
the career path . . . toward flipping burgers.

•

52. You need to know some
decisions you make in college
will impact the rest of your life.

53. You need to know that if you've read one hundred good books before showing up on campus, even math and science classes will be easier.

•

54. You need to know good grades won't magically appear just because you feel like you worked hard.

•

55. You need to know how to do research. Not just "ask your mom research," but hard, diligent, frustrating, time-consuming research. Like you did when tracking down that redhead's name and number.

56. You need to know
how to concentrate on reading
a textbook regardless of the
background noise. This skill alone
can propel you to graduating with honors.

•

57. You need to know that
when your parents said, "You can
be anything you want to be," they
were humoring you. You were six.
You need to find out what you're good at.

•

58. You need to know to take personal
responsibility. Success or failure is now
based on your decisions and your effort.

59. You need to know classes fill up quickly. If you're at the beach while everyone else is registering for classes, you'll experience the joy of going to school at night and on weekends.

•

60. You need to know the term *major* has nothing to do with the military.

•

61. You need to know that no matter how brilliant you are, a host of other factors like discipline, organization, commitment, subject interest, and reading ability will influence your ability to learn.

•

62. You need to know that procrastination is a good way to torch the $15,000 or so this semester is costing your parents.

63. You need to know when to turn off the television. This skill pays dividends your freshman year.

•

64. You need to know loneliness, money problems, alcohol, and poor study habits kill college performance.

•

65. You need to know to buy your books before exams start. Especially the thick ones.

•

66. You need to know professors won't reschedule tests or papers because of an important sorority party.

67. You need to know you
can't turn in work that was due
four weeks ago. Your mother
calling the professor won't help.

•

68. You need to know the absolute
quickest way to alienate a professor
is to complain to the department
chair or dean about a grade.

•

69. You need to know your
college classes will be filled with
strange-looking people. Odds
are, you may be one of them.

70. You need to know your profs will not immediately respond to your e-mails. Especially the ones you send Sunday night about homework due Monday.

71. You need to know college is all about study habits and focus.

72. You need to know that the nerd in the corner of the library is going to be running a Fortune 500 company one day. Make friends.

73. You need to know your future employers aren't really going to care about your college social life. They'll want to see what you've learned and accomplished.

74. You need to know to find someone
to emulate who isn't in rehab.

•

75. You need to know if you're
spending more time thinking about your
tan and your abs than your mind, you'll
be out of school by the end of the year.

•

76. You need to know it's time to value
mental fitness over physical fitness.

•

77. You need to know professors don't
have to get along with you. You have
to learn to get along with them.

•

78. You need to know how to create
a homework schedule and daily planner.
These are the tools of college graduates.

79. You need to know not to get upset when college ceases to be fun.

•

80. You need to know to attend freshman orientation camp—or whatever it's called. Yes, you will probably sit in some "Kum Ba Yah" circle and play stupid name games, and you can already tell it won't be cool, but on the first day of school, you'll actually know people. And that *is* cool.

•

81. You need to know it's time to start reading biographies of esteemed politicians, spiritual leaders, and successful businesspeople. These are the people you want to be like.

•

82. You need to know the term *bachelor* has nothing to do with single men.

83. You need to know your goal. It's hard enough to pull your fifth all-nighter of the quarter, so have some idea of what you're working for.

•

84. You need to know you're more likely to finish your degree faster if you start at a small private college instead of at a state school.

•

85. You need to know small private colleges look more expensive, but they often come with more grants, scholarships, and loans than state schools do.

•

86. You need to know it takes longer to graduate from a large state university— sometimes six years—because some required classes have a one-year waiting list.

87. You need to know the educational
path required to accomplish your
career goals. You're not going to get into
dental school majoring in political science.

·

88. You need to know two words
if you have no idea what you want
to do in five years: liberal arts.

·

89. You need to know a liberal arts degree
has nothing to do with art or drawing or
being a Democrat. (Yes, it's confusing.)

·

90. You need to know most applicants
are turned down by schools like Harvard,
University of Texas, and Duke University.
Don't let a rejection by one school
affect your performance at another.

91. You need to know that being accepted by even your thirtieth choice of colleges says something important: this school believes you'll graduate.

92. You need to know the whole point of college: better job opportunities.

93. You need to know that if you pick a college with two hundred kids per class, you can get emotionally, mentally, and physically lost.

94. You need to know the worst reason to choose a school is because your high-school flame is going there. The odds are high that one of you will leave.

95. You need to know that every year you dally in college is one year of full-time income you lose in the job market. That makes college even more expensive.

•

96. You need to know it doesn't matter if you go to a big college or a small college if your head isn't screwed on straight. You'll be out in a year.

•

97. You need to know that few freshmen are prepared for the amount of work college demands outside of class.

•

98. You need to know that if your $400-a-month food allowance lasts about a week, Dad won't understand.

99. You need to know it doesn't matter if you were popular, a Goth, a geek, or a cheerleader in high school. You're now a freshman.

•

100. You need to know that many of the most valuable life lessons will happen far away from the classroom. Lessons like choosing between going to work so you can pay rent or studying so you can keep your scholarship. They are experiences that forge adulthood.

•

101. You need to know that graduating with a baccalaureate degree is going to take a four- or five-year commitment that many young adults aren't mature enough to make.

102. You need to know to register for fifteen hours per term. That's a full load but not impossible, and if you have to drop a class, you won't go into academic probation or become financially ineligible.

•

103. You need to know the most important thing you can pack isn't your iPod, TV, stereo, or cell phone. It's a laptop. You'll be at a distinct disadvantage without one.

•

104. You need to know you can buy software—the really good stuff—at dirt cheap student prices. Check Apple.com or AcademicSuperstore.com.

•

105. You need to know the least important thing on campus is a car. Thousands and thousands of students survive without one.

106. You need to know to pack a
USB flash drive or two. You can back
up your work, copy notes from another
computer, and use it to print documents
at the computer center in the event you
drop your laptop off the balcony.

•

107. You need to know to call the
university and find out what computer
system its tech team supports. If you
show up with a computer it doesn't
support, you're on your own for four years.

•

108. You need to know to pack a month of
underwear. Everyone with be grateful. And you
won't be sent home with some strange rash.

109. You need to pack detergent.
If you don't know why or how
to use it, talk to your mother.

•

110. You need to know to go to all the
freshman orientations. Even if it means
touring the campus for the fifth time,
you'll learn names, see faces, and figure
out who can help you when you need it.
Plus, after five orientations, you may
actually learn your way around campus.

•

111. You need to know how to wake up
without your mother yelling at you. Or
you'll soon be back at home listening to her.

•

112. You need to know the first
semester is the hardest.

You Need to Know Your Roommate Might Smell

113. You need to know to send in your
dorm reservation as soon as you get accepted.
On-campus housing fills up quickly.

•

114. You need to know to live in the dorm.
It's the easiest way to make friends, feel
connected to the school, and avoid flunking out.

•

115. You need to know you're
moving into a dorm built fifty
years ago, not a condo built last week.

•

116. You need to know all your clothes,
pillows, quilts, towels, medicine, grooming
aids, hair products, blankets, sheets, radio,
computer, TV, shoes, and minibar have to
fit into a space the size of a MINI Cooper.

117. You need to know your roommate might emit an odor. Or have a gas problem. This is no reason to turn around and go home.

•

118. You need to know to never use your roommate's dirty towel or razor. Yes, you're dripping wet and your date is in thirty minutes, but, dude, staph is forever.

•

119. You need to know your roommate will be different from you. But she's somebody to talk to at 1:00 a.m. with the lights off.

•

120. You need to know a roommate teaches tolerance. Of course, you'll be teaching her tolerance too.

121. You need to know your roommate will probably never be your best friend. That's okay. Your friends don't want to live with you.

•

122. You need to know living with your best friend from high school can make you wish you were living with your little sister.

•

123. You need to know you won't have a private bathroom. In fact, you could share a bathroom with twenty or so people.

•

124. You need to know a coed dorm will quickly take the mystery out of the opposite sex.

125. You need to know the
most important shower accessory
is a pair of Crocs or flip-flops. What's
living on those floors can stop an army.

•

126. You need to know to not worry
whether or not your roommate likes
you. Find reasons to like your roommate.

•

127. You need to know kids who live
in the dorms make higher grades.

•

128. You need to know a dorm is
the cheapest housing around for miles.
Unaffordable housing means you have
to work part-time jobs longer just
to afford a roof over your head.

129. You need to know to not
be the last one to move into a
three-person dorm room.

•

130. You need to know roommates
get upset when you do things like
leave your fingernails in the sink.

•

131. You need to know you
can't change anybody by getting
mad or arguing. Even if that
person sleeps three feet above you.

•

132. You need to know husbands
and wives fight, brothers and sisters
fight, and roommates fight. Don't let
a misunderstanding send you home.

133. You need to know that, in many states, if you get into a fistfight with your roommate, you can be charged with domestic violence. Weird, but true.

•

134. You need to know whether you and your roommate need rules. Like rules about borrowing makeup, playing Halo 3 at 4:00 a.m., passing gas more than three times an hour. Rules help with these things.

•

135. You need to know courtesy helps when everything else fails.

•

136. You need to know college dorm beds are smaller than your bed at home.

137. You need to know it takes about three months to adjust to dorm life.

•

138. You need to know that living off campus can be really isolating, and isolation brings even the most independent kids home.

•

139. You need to know one of the best predictors for dropping out of college is how far away from campus you live. Those living closest do the best.

•

140. You need to know your RA (resident assistant). If she likes you, you can get away with just about anything.

141. You need to know to go to your RA if your roommate is from hell. In extreme cases, colleges will move you around.

•

142. You need to know applying the Golden Rule helps immensely with roommates.

•

143. You need to know the importance of duct tape. You'll understand when you get there.

•

144. You need to know to not get hung up trying to remodel your dorm room. It's a dorm room, it's small, it's thirty years old, it's heinous. Accept it.

•

145. You need to know to lock your room when you go down the hall to pee. Even at night.

146. You need to know your roommate may not share your fondness for Puff Daddy or Twisted Sister. Pack your iPod.

•

147. You need to know that no one is going to feel sorry for you if you lose your room key.

•

148. You need to know you can personalize your dorm room door with pictures, messages, poems, and drawings. It's how students tell other students who's behind the closed door.

•

149. You need to know to leave your dorm door open when you're in.
An open door is an invitation to other students to stick their head in and say hello.

You Need to Know the First Two Weeks Help Determine the Next Four Years

150. You need to know the more
people you meet in the first couple
of weeks, the greater your chances
of staying put and getting your degree.

•

151. You need to know meeting people is
never easier than during your first fourteen
days. Everybody is anxious to make friends.

•

152. You need to know that who
your friends are will have a direct
influence on your success at college.

•

153. You need to know you can
often avoid a lot of prerequisite
courses by getting a random form signed
by some administrator or professor.

154. You need to know that the good-looking blonde sitting beside you is shy too. Introduce yourself.

•

155. You need to know a freshman survival course might be the key to graduating in four years. It will teach you how to write a term paper, make friends, manage your time, and study.

•

156. You need to know to join everything that's meeting the first two weeks: clubs, student organizations, volunteer groups, Greeks, whatever. Thinking you're too cool to join anything will assure you a short, lonely college experience.

157. You need to know not to
feel ostracized or excluded because
you don't know people. No one knows
anybody. Except the upperclassmen.

•

158. You need to know there's no way
you can look any stupider in class than
the other freshmen. Unless you show up in
your pajamas. Then you'll look stupider.

•

159. You need to know a lot of
college students have acne. Don't let
that keep you from meeting people.

•

160. You need to know it's perfectly fine
to party till 3 o'clock every morning as
long as you have the stamina and if you
studied for six hours that afternoon.

•

161. You need to know college isn't as easy as it seems the first week. Start studying now or you'll be three chapters behind by the second week.

•

162. You need to know to start getting As quickly.

•

163. You need to know that, as of now, you'll make decisions every day that affect whether or not you will get your degree.

•

164. You need to know the lines at the bookstore will stretch to China the first two or three days. This is not an excuse for showing up in class without books. It's a reason to show up at the bookstore early.

165. You need to know to make friends in your classes. It helps to have people to compare notes with.

•

166. You need to know freshmen get the crappy parking spots.

•

167. You need to know the school makes a lot of money off freshmen who park illegally in order to get to class on time.

•

168. You need to know where your classes are before school starts. This small gesture says, "Hey, I have a brain and I'm using it!"

•

169. You need to know where your classroom is, not just the building. Room 4–345W v1.1 could be in the basement. Or maybe it's on the top floor. Or across campus.

170. You need to know to not schedule back-to-back classes a half mile apart.

•

171. You need to know it's okay to ask other students where the science building is.

•

172. You need to know to not make a scene if you find yourself sitting in the wrong classroom. Just take notes, act like you belong, and find the right classroom after the period ends.

•

173. You need to know that professors will post the semester's reading assignments, term papers, and exams online and/or hand them out in class. This gold mine of information is called a syllabus. Make a copy. Send it to your mother. Guard it with your life.

174. You need to know that a
syllabus isn't a list of suggestions.

•

175. You need to know that asking,
"What's due this Friday?" makes you
look like an idiot. Read your syllabus.

•

176. You need to know the "I didn't know
it was due" excuse that might have worked in
high school won't work now. Really. Don't
try it. You'll be laughed out of class.

•

177. You need to know that the dates
assigned for exams and papers are
what you now plan your life around.

178. You need to know that if
a class is too full for you to get
into, attend the first class anyway.
The professor just might squeeze you in.

•

179. You need to know you're now
living on self-discipline. Three weeks ago
Dad was telling you to be home early.

•

180. You need to know the newfound
freedom that college offers will
either make you or break you.

•

181. You need to know how to get yourself
organized. The way you spend your time and
energy will have a direct impact on whether or
not you make it to your sophomore year.

182. You need to know that if you
have a well-stocked refrigerator,
you'll never want for friends.

•

183. You need to know that
just because a professor looks at you
doesn't mean he's going to call on you.
However, looking down at your toenails
does tell him you don't know anything.

•

184. You need to know being on
time will keep you in college. Be on time
to class, with your assignments, with
your reading, with your papers, with
your forms, with your tuition checks.

185. You need to know the rules:
what gets you thrown out of a dorm;
what you need to do to graduate; what
behavior is acceptable and what isn't.
It's all there in your student handbook.

•

186. You need to know to meet with your
counselor two times a semester. That person
is paid to advise you on what major to pursue,
tell you what classes to take and to drop,
and help you resolve scheduling conflicts.

•

187. You need to know to call your counselor
before you call your parents. In fact, you probably won't be able to reach your parents. They're
off working second jobs to pay for college.

188. You need to know
to change counselors if you don't
click with yours. Think of this as
a chance to pick your parents.

·

189. You need to know to say
hello to those kids you recognize
from freshman camp. This is where that
goofy week begins to pay big dividends.

·

190. You need to know to not
make the mistake of thinking that
since you've gone to class, you're done
for the day. You're really just starting.

·

191. You need to know to get most
of your sleep in bed, not in class.

192. You need to know even a party school means lots of homework. Yes, it's called false advertising.

•

193. You need to know to visit the financial aid office and apply for grants or loans for the next semester even if you don't think you qualify. You never know.

•

194. You need to know the biggest mistake most students make is to not take advantage of their school's resources. Your tuition pays for all the health services, study assistance programs, tutors, career guidance officers, and other campus professionals. Use them.

195. You need to know to find a
place for studying. It could be Starbucks.
Or behind the stacks at the college library.
Or your dorm room. You need a place where
your brain realizes it's time to get serious.

•

196. You need to know it's important
to develop a relationship with your
professor now, not a week before exams
and when you're not sure what a cosine is.

•

197. You need to know to develop a
balance between studying and playing,
sleeping and exercising, meeting new people
and forming relationships. Kids who keep
everything in balance wind up with degrees.

198. You need to know to join a study group. You'll meet people—and some studying might actually break out.

•

199. You need to know to visit the writing lab before turning in a paper. Odds are slim you learned how to write college papers in high school.

•

200. You need to know the campus workout center is where you'll meet people who are in really good shape (not that you're that shallow) and where you can burn off the frustrations of chemistry lab.

201. You need to know that when
your brain is wasted from calculus,
it's either time to kill space aliens, go to
the tanning booth, or catch up on sleep.

•

202. You need to know if you hang out with
emotional basket cases, you'll become one.

•

203. You need to know that
studying is job #1.

•

204. You need to know procrastination
will guarantee your seat being filled
by another student next semester.

•

205. You need to know the
nerds win in the end.

You Need to Know
Choosing a Major Is
More Crucial to
Future Financial
Success Than
Choosing a College

206. You need to know that choosing the right major is often the key to getting the preferred internships, gaining admittance into the highest-rated graduate programs, and landing the highest starting salary in your field.

·

207. You need to know the earlier you choose a major, the more likely you are to graduate in four years. The reason is, all majors require courses designed to be taken in sequence over a four-year period—and often only those who have declared the major can get those classes.

208. You need to know tools like
the Myers-Briggs Type Indicator can
help point you in the right direction
for choosing your major. Talk to
someone at the career guidance center.

•

209. You need to know declaring a major
will make choosing classes a lot easier.

•

210. You need to know to take a
number of different courses to see what
you like if you have absolutely no idea
what to major in. You may have a latent
ability for science and not know it.

•

211. You need to know deciding
on a major scares most students because it
involves making a long-term commitment.

212. You need to know what's going on today in your fields of interest. Visit career centers, Web sites, professional journals, career fairs. Talk to different people in each field.

•

213. You need to know that just because you like playing computer games doesn't mean you have the smarts for a computer science degree.

•

214. You need to know you're being asked to choose your life's work before, according to scientists, your brain is fully formed. That's why people find themselves in the second year of law school hating law.

215. You need to know to not listen
to all that nonsense about college
being a time of "personal exploration."
At up to $50,000 a year, it's job training.

•

216. You need to know to not
be afraid to change your major if
you can't pass the required classes.
You may dream of a pre-med degree,
but if your highest grade in biology is 19,
you're never going to be a doctor. Move on.

•

217. You need to know that your
school will track your degree progress.
If you can't do the course work in a certain
major, they'll change your major for you.

218. You need to know it's perfectly
okay to check the "undecided" box next
to the word *major* when you enroll. You have
a couple of years to find the field of study
that makes you want to get up in the morning.

•

219. You need to know to just choose a major
and graduate if, by your third year, you have no
idea what you want to do. According to
a British study, around 40 percent of the jobs
available to new graduates are open
to people with a degree in any subject.

•

220. You need to know that if you want
to be a doctor, architect, or engineer,
not to waste your time taking classes
designed for a political science major.

221. You need to know that a major requires specific courses, and a grad school requires a different set of specific courses. The difference between the two can mean three more years of undergraduate work.

•

222. You need to know to not let current market conditions dictate your degree choices. What's hot today could be stone cold in four years. Ask any computer engineer.

•

223. You need to know that one way to decide on a major is to list the degrees you can never in a million years see yourself earning. Now you have a much shorter list to agonize over.

•

224. You need to know that personality, aptitude, interest, and values are as important as a starting salary when you're choosing a major.

225. You need to know that
borrowing $175,000 to become a
social worker will lead to economic ruin.

•

226. You need to know to use summer internships and missionary work to explore degree
ideas. Go to Romania with a dental mission
team. You may find you love yanking teeth.

•

227. You need to know to make sure you
get an adviser in your major's department
and check in regularly. She can help identify
those classes that are vital to your degree
plan, but are offered only once a year.

•

228. You need to know that every time you
change your major after your junior year, you
add at least one year to your graduation date.

You Need to Know How to Choose Classes

229. You need to know to take classes that will help you meet your graduation requirements. Forgetting this is why kids spend six years in college and leave with $400-a-month student loan payments—and no degree.

•

230. You need to know that if you avoid math classes in college, you're making the decision to not pursue medical school, law school, or an MBA. They all require advanced math.

•

231. You need to know to not choose classes because your best friend is taking them. You may not be aware that she actually finds organic chemistry fascinating.

232. You need to know
that, to any company, your
value goes up exponentially if
you speak another language.

•

233. You need to know that even
liberal arts and philosophy majors
can use some business courses.

•

234. You need to know there are
different pathways in each industry.
Hollywood has its money people and
its creative people, health care has its
doctors and administrators, high tech has
its engineers and its marketing people.

235. You need to know some
professors give only one or
two of their students an A.

•

236. You need to know to
ask older students about professors.
They are happy to share war stories.

•

237. You need to know to jump at any
opportunity to study in a foreign country.

•

238. You need to know about
www.ratemyprofessor.com and
www.pickaprof.com. See how other students
from your school graded the professors.

239. You need to know that
the university's most famous
professors may be the worst teachers.

•

**240. You need to know that if
you find a professor you like,
take as many courses as you can
from her that relate to your major.**

•

241. You need to know to not
pick a professor because he's the
funniest person on campus. Pick a prof
whose students go on to get great jobs.

242. You need to know that
some of your most valuable classes
will not be fun. In fact, they will
make you want to call your mother.
These classes will also, however, be
instrumental in getting you into
graduate school and then into a great job.

•

243. You need to know to occasionally
ask your professors—respectfully—
how their classes relate to the other classes
you're taking. If there's no relationship,
you need to chat with your adviser.

244. You need to know you can't
tell what a class covers by its name.
In some schools, "Communication 101"
refers to a television production class,
and in other schools it has to do
with speech and hearing problems.

•

245. You need to know if you
have to ask what Chemical Processing
is, you don't need to sign up for it.

•

246. You need to know that pass/fail
courses are not easier. Quite often students
who aim at just passing don't take the course
seriously, end up blowing it, wind up ruining
their GPA, and take the class again next semester. And have to try to explain things to Dad.

247. You need to know to try
to not schedule classes on Friday
morning if you can get away with it.
For some odd reason, a lot of college
parties happen Thursday night.

·

248. You need to know the evening
classes are sometimes easier. Maybe
because by 8 o'clock at night the
professors are as tired as their students.

·

249. You need to know that
just because you bombed biology in ninth
grade doesn't mean you can't handle
biology in college. You'll be amazed at
what determination and maturity can do.

You Need to Know How to Survive Campus Life

250. You need to know that everyone
is scared to death about fitting in.
You're no different. Well, your hair is
different. But outside of that . . .

•

251. You need to know you will embarrass yourself at least once a month. But everybody else is
so embarrassed themselves, they won't notice.

•

252. You need to know to talk to anyone
and everyone—to the person waiting outside
the lecture hall, sitting in the cafeteria,
walking next to you as you cross campus.

•

253. You need to know to not
try to impress everyone you meet.

•

254. You need to know to not let another person's
shyness throw you. Introduce yourself.

255. You need to know your campus bookstore has everything you need to get through your classes. But its prices may rival Neiman Marcus.

•

256. You need to know to not leave your clothes in the dorm's dryer overnight. You don't want to have to explain to your mom that everything you own has been stolen.

•

257. You need to know most colleges offer free transportation between dorms, student apartments, and classes. Of course, telling the professor you missed the bus will just attract unwanted attention.

•

258. You need to know professors can help you land campus jobs, smooth admission into required classes, and put you back on track when class work begins to kick your butt.

259. You need to know if your grades are substandard, it's even more critical for you to take advantage of college internships and leadership positions in extracurricular activities.

•

260. You need to know to watch your language. Anything racist, sexist, or threatening can have you thrown out.

•

261. You need to know it's not okay for professors to hit on you.

•

262. You need to know hitting on professors isn't advisable either.

•

263. You need to know your GPA. It's how you're measured against everyone else on campus.

264. You need to know where
the campus computer center is. Between
classes, you can work on papers, print out
homework, and e-mail your parents for money.

•

265. You need to know that the computer center
contains viruses that could stop the Defense
Department's computers. Handle with care.

•

266. You need to know the campus tutoring center
is the place to go if you can't figure out a chemistry
problem or answer a homework question.

•

267. You need to know the most important
office on campus is the Registrar's Office.
They are the people who keep all your
academic and personal records and who also
determine who graduates when by deciding
who takes classes when. Go bearing gifts.

268. You need to know your college offers workshops on everything from speed-reading to writing marketing plans. Take advantage of them. They're cheap, if not free.

•

269. You need to know that your college regularly sponsors lectures by some of the most important people in the world. Attending them is a great way to understand there's more to life than the next kegger.

•

270. You need to know your classmates care more about how you smell than how you look.

•

271. You need to know academic clubs like the Biology Club or the Pre-med Club or the Marketing Club are key to meeting contacts who lead to job offers. While your classmates are off sun tanning, you can be networking.

272. You need to know dropping
or changing a class is so involved,
you might as well just read the textbook.

•

273. You need to know to whom, where, and
when to turn in your FAFSA (Free Application
for Federal Student Aid) forms every year.

•

274. You need to know where to find
the undergraduate adviser. Before you
start slipping through the cracks.

•

275. You need to know how to
contact campus security if you
want a late-night escort to your car.

276. You need to know your biorhythms. Can you function well at 8:00 a.m., or are you better off starting with a 10:00 a.m. class?

•

277. You need to know how to navigate the library search engine. You're going to need things like call numbers, subject headings, etc. You're not in Google anymore.

•

278. You need to know how to use every tool in the library. Before your first research paper is due.

•

279. You need to know to not just sit around in your dorm and feel alone. Get out.

280. You need to know that you have
to enroll for classes every semester. Do it early
and you'll get the classes you want. Do it late
and your kids may graduate before you do.

•

281. You need to know that to enroll for
future classes, you'll need a computer and
an alarm clock. Classes fill up by 6:15 a.m.

•

282. You need to know e-mailing the professors
before registration sometimes leads to class
positions miraculously being held open for you.

•

283. You need to know that changing your
major, dealing with a campus parking ticket,
or replacing a student ID means facing a
bureaucratic labyrinth. Without Mom and Dad.

284. You need to know you're not a
failure even though no one has paid
you a compliment in the last thirty days.
They're hard to come by in college.

•

285. You need to know that going to
bed early often means midnight; 3 a.m.
is typical; 4:30 a.m. is "Why bother?"

•

286. You need to know if you like
writing, don't just sit in your apartment
wearing a dark coat like Dostoyevsky.
Join the campus newspaper or magazine.

•

287. You need to know some classes require so
many papers and projects you will see no way of
getting everything done. Just remember, dumber
students have gone before you and made it.

288. You need to know to accept responsibility for going to the all-night toga party and not writing your paper. Don't expect professors to be sympathetic.

•

289. You need to know that the kid who always gets a B- while you always get a C+ on the same work has made friends with the professor.

•

290. You need to know the administration and the faculty's office staff. They're the ones who can find you fifteen minutes on a prof's calendar.

•

291. You need to know asking your professor to change your semester grade because it's not an A won't work. And it won't work any better if your mother calls.

292. You need to know you can form good habits simply by practicing them daily.

•

293. You need to know someone to talk to about each of your classes. Another reason to make friends.

•

294. You need to know to read anything that shows up from the university in your e-mail or mailbox.

•

295. You need to know a cheap bike is a great way to get around campus without worrying about parking tickets. You'll also be able to get closer to your classrooms.

•

296. You need to know real-life tragedies happen on campus. You can be assaulted, fall down stairs, be involved in a wreck, get your wallet stolen. Stay aware. And have a plan.

You Need to Know
How to Survive
College Classes

297. You need to know to go to class. Seriously. It's the key to getting a degree.

•

298. You need to know to go to class even if you don't have your homework done. Or if you're hung over. Or if you're sick as a dog. Go to class.

•

299. You need to know most college professors are proud, opinionated, arrogant, accomplished, and don't really care if you pass or fail. It's their world, and you're taking up space in it.

•

300. You need to know some professors automatically fail students for missing only 15 percent of their classes. Unless your parents can write a huge check to the alumni fund.

301. You need to know it's a myth that attendance isn't taken in college. Many colleges require it.

•

302. You need to know it's as important to learn the instructor as it is to learn the material.

•

303. You need to know if the professor talks about something not in the book, you will be tested on it.

•

304. You need to know you'll see questions on tests not covered in class. Professors love to see if you've been reading.

•

305. You need to know professors drop hints in their lectures about what will be on the test. If you're trying to make eye contact with that cute redhead, you can miss this.

306. You need to know the core vocabulary used in each class. If the professor seems to be speaking a foreign language, drop the course and take a primer.

•

307. You need to know you could have two hours of reading tonight. Per class.

•

308. You need to know that all the information you need for writing research papers cannot be found on the Internet. Take a library orientation course.

•

309. You need to know you can't get a homework deadline extended by e-mailing your professor with a question the night before. This tactic didn't work in 1995.

310. You need to know to read your assignments before class. The professor's lecture will make a lot more sense.

•

311. You need to know that if a class is putting you to sleep, get a double espresso beforehand.

•

312. You need to know to finish homework two days before it's due, not the hour before. This gives you time to review it and make corrections.

•

313. You need to know the best students don't actually enjoy every minute of studying. They struggle too.

•

314. You need to know that if you don't really comprehend the fundamentals of what you're studying, call a tutor. Before the final.

•

315. You need to know that even if an assignment is worth only 1 percent of your grade, you'll be grateful for every single percent you've racked up come the end of the semester.

•

316. You need to know to study your hardest subjects first. Calculus makes even less sense when your brain is tired.

•

317. You need to know you can do everything right and still get a B from your professor.

•

318. You need to know partial credit beats no credit. Turn in your homework even if it's late.

•

319. You need to know that dazzling concepts will be presented every day without any dazzling special effects. If you have a short attention span, you're sunk.

320. You need to know to study the same subject at the same time for the same amount of time every day. This is called discipline. It's how people earn As.

•

321. You need to know there's a difference between critical thinking and memorization. You can memorize a girl's phone number. Critical thinking is analyzing whether or not she will be seen with you.

•

322. You need to know there's nothing like a couple of zeros on pop quizzes—because you were absent from class—to quickly bring down your grade.

323. You need to know if your professor has a course Web site. Many do. These sites typically have sample test questions, exam reviews, lists of additional reading material, and more.

•

324. You need to know to address your professor as either "Doctor" or "Professor." Not "Miss." You're no longer in high school.

•

325. You need to know to not watch movies on your iPod during class.

•

326. You need to know to have an opinion and to share it in class. This tells the professor you're not dead.

327. You need to know professors expect
you to complete your assignments
on time. They won't argue about
a late paper. They'll just fail you.

•

328. You need to know that if you
ask your professor for a special appointment
because his office hours are inconvenient for
you, your name will go down on a list.

•

329. You need to know many professors
don't provide a list of study questions.

•

330. You need to know that buckling down
and getting your work done takes a lot less
time and stress than cramming all night.

•

331. You need to know you're toast if
you miss more than one math class.

332. You need to know to not smoke pot before class. Yes, it makes the next ninety minutes more interesting, but people will wonder what you find so funny about a frog dissection.

•

333. You need to know your typical workload will include at least one major paper, exam, or lab practical a week.

•

334. You need to know to do all your homework, even if you don't have to turn it in. It's how you learn.

•

335. You need to know professors hate having stupid questions asked in class. They'll think you're trying to be the center of attention.

336. You need to know some of your assignments won't be due for months. Waiting months to start them, though, will have you in community college next semester.

•

337. You need to know that getting one of the highest grades in class on a hard college test is one of the coolest experiences you will ever have. And it's totally worth the effort.

•

338. You need to know to not blame the professor because you're failing.

•

339. You need to know you can't keep all your assignments—what they are, when they're due—in your head. This is the same head that can't remember that hot blonde's name. And you think you can remember your chemistry assignments? Right . . .

340. You need to know to make flash cards for every course. Write down the key ideas and carry the cards around with you. These are sure conversation starters in bars.

•

341. You need to know you won't have time for a regular afternoon nap or tanning appointment.

•

342. You need to know your professor could be an atheist, a communist, a bigot, a feminist, or a sexist. Your job is still to make your grades.

•

343. You need to know which readings in your classes are crucial and which ones are optional. Students who don't know this study the wrong material for hours.

•

344. You need to know that sending ten text messages during class indicates you're missing the main points of a lecture.

345. You need to know you're
not entitled to a do-over.

•

346. You need to know to approach class
work like a job. Figure out how much time
you need to spend on your studies and consis-
tently spend that amount of time on them.

•

347. You need to know when it's
too late to ask questions. Like when
the exams are being passed out.

•

348. You need to know to not give up
when you learn you're not above average.

•

349. You need to know college is a lot
like the real world: some people can do
some things better with less effort.

350. You need to know to sit as
close to your professor as you can.
It's easier for her to start recognizing you.

•

351. You need to know your
professors won't praise you for a job
well done. They expect you to perform.

•

352. You need to know a B or C is
no reason to argue with your professor.
See it as a sign you need to work harder.

•

353. You need to know that if you store
your homework on a flash drive, you can work
on it at the computer center between classes.

•

354. You need to know studying
till 3:00 a.m. isn't unusual.

355. You need to know to strive for nerd-dom.
Nerds do better in college than non-nerds.

•

356. You need to know to look around your
class and remind yourself that you're not the
dumbest person in the room. Well, okay, maybe
you are. But you're not the dumbest person on
the floor. Okay, okay, but not the whole building.

•

357. You need to know that the
panicky, sickly feeling is your fear
of low grades. It's a common symptom.

•

358. You need to know professors want to
be the center of attention in their classroom.
They do not want to compete with e-mails,
text messaging, and Internet surfing.

•

359. You need to know to go to the library
and study between classes. Not go back to bed.

360. You need to know to start an
essay two weeks before it's due.
Not an hour before class.

•

361. You need to know that if
you've studied hard throughout the day,
you can be surfing YouTube at 10:00 p.m.
And still making your grades.

•

362. You need to know to study one
subject at time. Knock out calculus
before moving on to English lit.

•

363. You need to know Thanksgiving break is
actually the week when you're assigned three
papers, given four hundred pages of reading,
and told to be prepared for a major humanities
test the following Monday. Have fun.

364. You need to know about the restorative powers of caffeine. Especially for those mornings when it's 3:15, you still have twenty more pages to read, and class starts in five hours.

•

365. You need to know if you can't get to know the professor, get to know the TA (teaching assistant). You need someone on your side.

•

366. You need to know to never date the TA. Breakups can get messy.

•

367. You need to know to never get so inebriated you e-mail a professor a love note or a threat. You'll be home or in jail within forty-eight hours.

•

368. You need to know a second-semester class builds on the first semester. If you weren't paying attention in October, you'll be sunk in January.

369. You need to know to not wear
flip-flops and gym shorts to class in
thirty-degree weather so you can look
cool. You'll look hung over. Or stupid.

•

370. You need to know you could spend
twenty hours writing a paper and receive the
same grade another student received who only
spent five hours. It's fair. It's life. Don't argue.

•

371. You need to know to talk with
your professor as soon as possible about
the topic of your writing assignment.
He may hate your first ten ideas.

•

372. You need to know that if you wait until
exam week to get a tutor, you've waited too long.

373. You need to know that if you
need to see a tutor every week, odds
are you've picked the wrong major.

•

374. You need to know professors
have no interest in helping you if you
haven't been coming to class all semester.

•

375. You need to know to study
with someone smarter than you.

•

376. You need to know there are Web sites that
can help you succeed. Freetranslation.com and
college-cram.com are some of the cooler ones.

•

377. You need to know if you're
not making As, don't give up.
Grad schools and employers like Bs too.

378. You need to know you can sometimes get an extension on a paper if you meet with the professor early enough. It helps to wear a sling. And bandages.

•

379. You need to know to not get discouraged by your first-semester grades. It takes a while for most students to find their legs.

•

380. You need to know to fearlessly dump a class if you're royally screwing it up. Although an expensive option (often you still have to pay for the class), this tactic can at least save your GPA.

•

381. You need to know that you need to actually learn what you were taught in class today. Learn the vocabulary, understand the chart, decipher the equation—don't go back to the dorm until you understand it.

You Need to Know How to Read for Content When There Are No Pictures

382. You need to know to at
least read the intro, conclusion,
headings, and highlights.

•

383. You need to know how to
find the main idea. Of a textbook.
Or a novel. Or an article.

•

384. You need to know how to
recognize material that will be covered
on a test. Things like highlighted
text, questions posed in margins,
diagrams, pictures, and tables. They're
all shouting, "This could be on the test!"

•

385. You need to know the glossary
of terms if you're to have any idea
what the textbook is talking about.

386. You need to know to
recognize information that could be
turned into a multiple-choice question.

•

387. You need to know
any information found on a
chart could be on a test.

•

388. You need to know anything
numbered or bulleted could be on a test.

•

389. You need to know that definitions
of key terms may not be on a test, but
will be critical to solving test problems.

390. You need to know that while
we're all proud of you for reading your
textbook, you now have to read it again.

•

391. You need to know to read
the chapter the professor is going
to talk about before class. It's a way
to avoid that dazed and confused
look that tells the professor you
have no idea what he's talking about.

•

392. You need to know that literature
requires you to, every now and then, stop
and think about what you're reading.
Is the author serious? Is it a satire?
Is it a dream? Do you have any idea?

You Need to Know How to Take Notes When You Can Barely Understand the Professor

393. You need to know taking
notes will help you pay attention—
which is, of course, the . . . uh . . . point.

•

394. You need to know if you
can't read your handwriting now,
there's no way you'll decipher
it at the end of the semester.

•

395. You need to know the Cornell
Method for taking notes. Draw a
1 1/2-inch margin on the left. Take
notes on the right side of the paper
and add questions pertaining
to the notes on the left side.

396. You need to know to
set up a binder for each class
you're taking. Mixing economic
notes with notes on Voltaire
can only lead to academic ruin.

•

397. You need to know to
take notes even when you record
lectures. If you can't understand the
professor in person, there's no way
you'll know what he's saying on tape.

•

398. You need to know to file
in your binder every day all the
class notes, text summary notes,
and papers your professor hands out.
Do this so you don't lose anything.

399. You need to know to read
over your notes before class starts.
Professors have a way of assuming
you're on the same page with them.

•

**400. You need to know that if
your professor says something
more than once, she's all but
telling you, "This will be on the test."**

•

401. You need to know to create
headings for each lecture and subheadings
for topics covered throughout.
This makes reviewing your notes
at exam time much easier.

402. You need to know to underline key statements, highlight important points, and use the margins to write summaries. If you don't know how to do this, take a class that will teach you.

•

403. You need to know to type your notes on your computer after every class before you do anything else. Now this information is filed in your computer, organized for exams, and possibly implanted in your brain.

•

404. You need to know to number and date each page of notes you take. You also need to know to not try to write down every word. Put the lecture in your own words.

405. You need to know to leave spaces between lines and double spaces between ideas. Your notes will be easier to review later.

•

406. You need to know to copy down everything your professor writes on the board.

•

407. You need to know whether your professors post their lecture notes on the Internet. If so, you've just gotten lucky. Print them out and stick them in your binder. Bring them to the lecture.

•

408. You need to know that if you take good notes in classes like government, history, and philosophy, the professor all but writes your paper for you.

You Need to Know to Work Nice in Groups

409. You need to know that
no matter how much you hate
working with other people, you
will be assigned group projects.

•

410. You need to know this
isn't the time to act like a loner
or a know-it-all or an entitled snot.
Your group will quickly shut you out.

•

411. You need to know to take the
lead. Most people will be grateful.

412. You need to know that, as dorky as it sounds, you need to create a group charter that outlines the goals and objectives of the group. If the goal is to get knee-walking drunk every Tuesday, write it down. If it's to figure out the subatomic particles circling Pluto, write that down.

•

413. You need to know the key to working successfully in any group is clear communication. Hoping people will work according to your moods won't work.

•

414. You need to know to set in stone when and where your group will meet.

415. You need to know what gets a person kicked out of the group.

•

416. You need to know how to defuse the inevitable tensions that arise in a group of people hitting their peak hormone levels at the same time.

•

417. You need to know that some of your ideas will not be enthusiastically received by others. Don't call their mother names.

•

418. You need to know how to defend your position without getting emotional. It's good practice for the real world.

419. You need to know
it's possible other people
will have good ideas. Really.

•

420. You need to know one person
shouldn't be left to do all the work.

•

421. You need to know the
strengths of each person in the group.
The math whiz probably shouldn't
be charged with writing the paper.

•

422. You need to know
to set deadlines. This avoids
last-minute meltdowns.

423. You need to know how to compromise. (If you have a little brother or sister, you know how.)

•

424. You need to know your group could have a few dysfunctional members. Families have them and survive. Project groups do too.

•

425. You need to know the quickest way to break up a group is to gossip about its members.

•

426. You need to know cutting class could impact your group's grade. They won't be amused.

You Need to Know That College Papers Are Longer Than Half a Page

427. You need to know how to
write papers and lab reports well.
Really, really well.

•

428. You need to know nothing says, "Last
minute" like a poorly written paper.

•

429. You need to know to pack
The Elements of Style by William Strunk Jr.
and E. B. White. It's your best hope of
getting through freshman comp.

•

430. You need to know to not
wait for a paper to be assigned to start
writing. Keep a journal, start a novel,
compose a love letter. Start writing.

431. You need to know to utilize the campus writing center. It's staffed with grad students trained to help you with writer's block, grammar, style, tone, and clarity. They are not, however, there to write your papers for you.

•

432. You need to know to take every paper to the writing center for review and critiquing before you turn it in.

•

433. You need to know what the specific assignment is. Nothing's worse than spending days writing about the wrong thing.

•

434. You need to know some science teachers will grade your lab reports down for poor grammar and typos.

435. You need to know the phases
of writing a paper:

- You need to develop the concept. If
your concept is dumb, your paper
doesn't have a prayer.

- You need to conduct research. This
step will require more time than the
TV commercials during *24*.

- You need to define your thesis. The
writing lab you stroll by every day—
you can find help there.

- You need to draft the outline. This
seems pointless, repetitive, and dumb.
You also can't do a paper without it.

- You need to write the first draft. This is where you put all your thoughts down on paper.

- You need to know only a moron would turn in the first draft. You'll get an F and be heavily ridiculed by the professor.

- You need to edit, revise, and polish the draft.

- Now you have a paper.

•

436. You need to know to allow yourself enough time. Lots of time. Time you'd rather be sleeping, tanning, playing tennis, or texting that redhead in econ.

437. You need to know to never
write a paper using only Wikipedia.
You'll sound just like all the other losers.
Besides, half of that stuff is wrong.

•

**438. You need to know your college library
has the answers. That's why it's so big.**

•

439. You need to know that if your paper is
not properly footnoted, you're going to fail.

•

**440. You need to know www.bibme.org is
a free bibliography maker. Type in the title
of your book, the Web site you've been using,
or the journal you just quoted, and the site
will automatically give you the full citation.**

•

441. You need to know to set up regular
conferences with the professor to review
your progress. Start early in the semester.

442. You need to know that if your professor can't follow your train of thought, you're going to fail.

•

443. You need to know the value of tools like subheads.

•

444. You need to know to close your paper with your strongest argument.

•

445. You need to know to not let your perfectionism keep you from turning in your papers on time.

•

446. You need to know that if your paper isn't well written, you're going to fail.

447. You need to know that if your paper
doesn't make a point, you're going to fail.

•

**448. You need to know that if
another student has turned in your
paper before, you're going to fail.**

•

449. You need to know to finish your paper
at least three days before it's due. That will give
you time to proofread it. Again and again.

•

**450. You need to know to read your
finished paper out loud to someone else.**

•

451. You need to know the professor
isn't going to give you an A for effort.
She expects effort. She will give you an A
if she thinks your work is brilliant.

You Need to Know How to Take an Exam Without Freezing Up

452. You need to know when there
will be a test. It's there on your syllabus.

•

453. You need to know telling
a professor you didn't know there
would be a test will only label you
as a loser who lost his syllabus.

•

454. You need to know what pages
the test will cover. Many kids fail
because they carefully read, memorize,
and review the wrong chapters.

•

455. You need to know what type of
test you're studying for. Multiple choice?
Critical thinking? Essay? It helps
to know your format.

456. You need to know to not study in your dorm room or anyplace there's a bed, a computer, a thumping speaker, or a TV.

•

457. You need to know not to hang out with students who are freaking out over the test. Panic is contagious.

•

458. You need to know you're not going to have time to do a semester's worth of reading in one night.

•

459. You need to know exams can start early. Like four to five weeks after school starts.

•

460. You need to know there's no time limit on studying. You work as long as it takes you to gain understanding.

461. You need to know to write a summary—in your own words—of the course material you're going to be tested on. Make an outline of the key points in each chapter. The more you write, the more you'll learn.

•

462. You need to know to use your course outline when reviewing the material. It shows you how your professor was thinking when preparing the course. Chances are she'll structure the exam the same way.

•

463. You need to know the why of what you're studying. Being able to discuss the impact and significance of an event is as important as memorizing dates and facts. Maybe more important.

464. You need to know to start studying at least a week before a test. The A students started even earlier.

•

465. You need to know to go to the class review sessions. Consider them a gift from your professor.

•

466. You need to know how to study using a highlighter. But if you highlight the whole book, you will learn nothing.

•

467. You need to know to make a note card for each major theme and idea your professor covers in class. Transfer notes from class lectures and your textbook onto each card.

468. You need to know not to
expect an easy test. That expectation
has sent many college students home.

•

469. You need to know what works for you.
Flash cards, studying with a friend, hiding
in the library—learn what helps you learn.

•

470. You need to know how to
control your study environment.
If it's too quiet, leave. If it's too noisy,
leave. If it's too hot, find the thermostat.

•

471. You need to know to not lie to
yourself. Don't tell yourself you know the
material when you've only looked at it once.

472. You need to know to have someone quiz you. Sometimes this is called a study date. And you actually, well, study.

•

473. You need to know that cramming for tests and exams indicates you've been busy with something other than studying.

•

474. You need to know the key to successful cramming is memorization.

•

475. You need to know that if you have headaches and nausea, you're infected with test anxiety. Get up and study.

•

476. You need to know test anxiety can cause you to blank out during an exam. It's an excuse your parents might buy, but your professor won't.

477. You need to know to get your
act together the night before the exam.
Don't be running around the next morning
looking for pens, calculators, and books.

•

478. You need to know to sleep
before an exam. A tired brain means
incoherent thinking and writing.

•

479. You need to know to read all of the
instructions before you begin
taking a test. People who can't be
bothered with instructions fail.

•

480. You need to know whether you can make
notes on your exam. If you can, write down
the most crucial, most-likely-to-forget
information as soon as the exam starts.

481. You need to know to quickly skim the questions and jot down your initial thoughts.

•

482. You need to know that if you don't know the answer to the first question, don't agonize over it. Move on.

•

483. You need to know which questions count the most and then spend your time on those.

•

484. You need to know to show your work or line of reasoning. Even if you get the answer wrong, you may get partial credit.

•

485. You need to know neatness matters. If the grader can't follow your reasoning, you're sunk. And if you leave evidence of a cluttered mind, your grade will be affected.

486. You need to know to bring a watch.
Check your progress at fifteen-minute intervals.

·

487. You need to know that if the test is
harder than you imagined, don't panic.
Forget getting the A. Your goal is to survive.

·

488. You need to know that if other students
are finishing before you, it might well be they've
given up. Take as much time as you can.

·

489. You need to know to read the
questions carefully. You can earn a quick
F by answering questions not on the test.

490. You need to know it's critical to do well on the first exam. Or you'll be playing catch-up the rest of the semester.

•

491. You need to know the six most common kinds of essay questions—and the kind of organized response they call for:

- Definition
- Analysis
- Cause and effect
- Comparison-contrast
- Process
- Thesis and support

•

492. You need to know to look for key words in an essay question that indicate how you will organize your answer.

493. You need to know that, when answering essay questions, you'll need an introduction and a conclusion.

•

494. You need to know that spending a few hours at the writing lab can increase your ability to answer essay questions.

•

495. You need to know you'll be answering questions like this: "Civil War historian Andy Bellum once wrote, 'Blahblahblah blahed a blahblah, but of course if blahblah blahblah blahed the blah, then blahblahs are not blah but blahblah.' To what extent and in what ways is this statement true? How is it false?" If you're not prepared, even prayer won't help.

You Need to Know How to Take a Multiple-Choice Test Without Choosing "B" Every Time

496. You need to know college
multiple-choice tests require
the thinking skills of recognition,
synthesis, analysis, and application.
If you don't know what those
words mean, go back to high school.

•

497. You need to know reading a multiple-
choice test requires the same skills you
need to read a textbook. (And those
skills are light-years beyond what
you need to read text messages.)

•

498. You need to know whether
your college offers a learning skills
course. If so, you can get help in
learning to take multiple-choice tests.

499. You need to know to read the beginning of each multiple-choice question (called the stem) together with each possible answer. Sometimes you can rule out answers because, grammatically, they don't work with the stem.

•

500. You need to know how to study every part of the question stem—the subject, the verb, and the modifiers. That's how you'll understand what's really being asked.

•

501. You need to know to study old exams to see the difference between correct and incorrect answers. Sometimes it's a modifier.

502. You need to know that multiple-choice tests require more than merely recognizing true statements. They often require recognizing the right answer in the context of the question.

•

503. You need to know that multiple-choice questions sometimes require fine distinctions between correct and nearly correct statements. In other words, memorization won't help. Understanding does.

•

504. You need to know there's no magic in picking "C" if you don't know the answer. It's an urban myth.

505. You need to know sometimes a multiple-choice answer is so obvious you'll think it's wrong. Especially if you've been studying and know the material.

•

506. You need to know to double-check your answers. Don't just turn in your test because you're sick of it. Take the time to reread it.

•

507. You need to know to do the multiple-choice part of a test first. It can hold clues to the other exam questions.

•

508. You need to know time is of the essence. You could be asked to answer seventy questions in one hour. Sometimes two hundred questions in three hours.

509. You need to know whether you'll
be marked down for an incorrect answer.
If not, it pays to guess. If you are penalized,
answer only the questions you know.

•

**510. You need to know to answer
the easiest questions first. Then go
back and work on the harder ones.**

•

511. You need to know a trick for
dealing with multiple-choice tests:
eliminate the obviously wrong answers first.
Then concentrate on choosing between
the correct and almost-correct answers.

512. You need to know words such as *every, all, none, always,* and *never* indicate the correct answer must be an undisputed fact.

•

513. You need to know that, in the social sciences, absolutes are rare.

•

514. You need to know that words like *usually, often, generally, may,* and *seldom* are qualifiers that could indicate a true statement.

•

515. You need to know subheads from the textbook frequently show up in the questions, either in the stem or as the right answer.

516. You need to know to do an analysis
of each test after you get your grade.
Figure out why you missed certain questions.

•

517. You need to know to study
your graded multiple-choice exam
to understand the distinction between the
correct answer and the wrong alternatives.

•

518. You need to know that, on multiple-
choice tests, the answer may indeed
always be "B." Professors like to do that.

•

519. You need to know that sometimes
you just blow it. Pick up and move on.

You Need to Know Cheating and Plagiarism Can Get You Kicked Out...No Matter How Much Your Mother Complains

520. You need to know to bring
your character into the classroom.

•

521. You need to know that copying
something without attribution,
even if you find it on some Russian
Web site, is plagiarism.

•

522. You need to know if you and twenty
other students turn in a paper with the same
words, the professor will call it cheating.

•

523. You need to know if you and twenty
other students miss the same questions on
a test with the same wrong answers, the
professor will call that cheating too.

524. You need to know if you and twenty other students who are failing suddenly ace the next exam, the professor will suspect cheating.

•

525. You need to know that unless the professor tells you otherwise, sharing information is cheating.

•

526. You need to know that asking someone what was on a test could be called research. Taking a copy of the test into an exam . . . cheating.

•

527. You need to know that just because the whole class is getting away with cheating doesn't mean you'll get away with it too. And that's a weak excuse when you get caught.

528. You need to know to not turn in any paper you yourself didn't write.

·

529. You need to know that if you copied from a paper posted on the Internet, that's cheating.

·

530. You need to know that if you think your spiffy new iPhone will help you access the Internet and send e-mail during tests, you're right. You should also know professors collect phones before exams.

·

531. You need to know that if a high grade is important enough to sell your soul, it should be important enough to miss a party or two, stay up a little longer to study, and actually learn the material.

532. You need to know professors aren't idiots. They're now using tools such as turnitin.com that can spot a plagiarized paragraph copied from a Bulgarian Web site.

•

533. You need to know that the last thing you want to lose is your professors' trust. If they catch you once, they'll always assume you're guilty.

•

534. You need to know college courses build on themselves. If you have to cheat to pass Biology 101, you're going to be sunk the next semester.

•

535. You need to know the penalties for cheating get stiffer (and more public) the higher you climb the college ladder.

536. You need to know to avoid
Web sites like cheathouse.com or planetpa-
pers.com. Yes, you can buy
a term paper online, but ethics aside,
they are so poorly written you're still
going to fail. And you'll be caught, and
you'll look like a loser at the same time.

•

537. You need to know to cite
everything you quote or copy in your
papers. Everything. And if you don't know
how, go to the writing center to learn.

•

538. You need to know that if you have
your act together, you don't have to cheat.
Allow plenty of time, do your paper in stages,
work with the writing center—it's that simple.

You Need to Know Transferring Can Make You Feel Like a Freshman All Over Again

539. You need to know transferring
schools is a hassle, and unless it's done for
reasons of health, finances, or a substantially
better college, it might not be worth it.

•

540. You need to know transferring schools is
a sure way to feel like an outsider. It'll be more
important than ever to meet people quickly.

•

541. You need to know that feelings of
loneliness will probably surface. You indeed
won't know anyone. But that can change.

•

542. You need to know the earlier
you decide to transfer schools, the better.
Find out what classes from your school
will transfer and sign up for those.

543. You need to know transfer shock can lead you to drop out. Instead of doing that, make a friend. Or talk to a counselor.

•

544. You need to know there are programs—like transition workshops, career planning workshops, or university experience courses—designed to help transfer students adjust.

•

545. You need to know other transfer students are as lost and confused as you are. Meet them through the Office of Student Affairs and other academic departments.

•

546. You need to know to join a group of some kind during your first week of classes. Even if you're not a freshman.

547. You need to know that a
lot of the credits you killed yourself
to earn at your old school may not
transfer to your new one. This is
what leads to six-year degree plans.

•

548. You need to know the introductory
classes you took at your old school may
not have prepared you for the advanced
classes at your new one. If so, swallow your
pride and take the intro classes again.

•

549. You need to know that if
you transferred because you're
involved with a person at your new
campus, you'll probably transfer again.

You Need to Know There's More to a Fraternity or Sorority Than Toga Parties (Well, a Little More)

550. You need to know fraternities
and sororities make it easy to meet people
and have an instant group of friends.

•

551. You need to know no one
thinks twice if you're not a Greek.
In fact, a lot of kids are opting out.

•

552. You need to know rush week
can make perfectly sane people nuts.
Especially girls and moms.

•

553. You need to know to be yourself.
Acting like somebody you're not will only
confuse everybody. Including you.

554. You need to know the whole point of all the rush parties is to meet people. Even if you don't pledge with them, these people can still be your friends.

•

555. You need to know the average GPA required of the fraternity you want to join. If it's around 2.5, you'll be hanging with a bunch of janitors. If it's around 3.8, you'll make friends with future CEOs.

•

556. You need to know that frat parties are memorable. If you can remember them.

•

557. You need to know that the Greek system offers great ways to get involved in campus leadership roles.

558. You need to know the food in a fraternity or sorority house is usually better than other campus offerings.

•

559. You need to know the Greek system attracts kids who like to party hardy. If you pledge, keep Betty Ford on your speed dial.

•

560. You need to know whether your fraternity has ever been written up for underage drinking. While that sounds fun, it means freshmen have been taken to the hospital after parties because they were vomiting their guts up. Not fun.

•

561. You need to know it's possible to join a fraternity and not drink. It's possible.

562. You need to know that, after
your sophomore year, a fraternity or
sorority might have outlived its usefulness.

•

563. You need to know that it's perfectly
okay to change your mind about joining
a frat. You don't have to stay stuck if
you realize you don't like the people.

•

564. You need to know if there's hazing.
Nothing's crazier than a bunch of
twenty-year-olds running torture sessions.

•

565. You need to know one key
draw to the Greek system is the housing.
It is often a better deal financially than
campus housing or apartments.

566. You need to know, according
to the US Department of Health,
joining a fraternity and sorority increases
your likelihood of graduation. Go figure.

•

567. You need to know a fraternity
or sorority isn't for the lazy. A number
of chapters do a lot of philanthropy.

•

568. You need to know that if a sorority
doesn't choose you for membership, they
were all medicated, boozy psychotics on
the verge of a breakdown. You're better off.

You Need to Know What Cool Things Could Convince You to Stay in School

569. You need to know some opportunities
to study abroad come with scholarships.

570. You need to know that
note-taking strategies are available
at the college's tutoring center.

571. You need to know that football,
basketball, and soccer games are where you
can scream, get crazy, and look no dumber
than the forty-year-old in the next section.
And your student ID will get you in cheap.

572. You need to know your school
has tunnels. You didn't read it here.

573. You need to know that
signing up for your school's most
bizarre class could keep you interested
in staying in school. It could be a study
of the compulsion to shop at 6:00 a.m.,
the impact Bob Dylan has had on plants,
or the effects of having Astroturf on
campus. Read your course offerings.

•

574. You need to know that
networking your butt off could
lead to meeting, say, the guy in
charge of sports programming for
one of the major networks. Or the
woman in charge of PR for a major
Hollywood studio. Happens every day.

575. You need to know some of
the biggest performers in the business
often hold concerts on college campuses.

•

576. You need to know to volunteer
on a university committee.

•

577. You need to know to take advantage
of all the incredible things on campus
you have already paid for: movie nights,
plays, guest speakers, museums, concerts,
newspapers, and sometimes cheap massages.

•

578. You need to know to take some
classes that have nothing to do with your
core or major: photography, creative writing,
TV production. Such a class could change
your entire attitude toward college.

579. You need to know you could be
a DJ at your campus radio station.

•

580. You need to know to sneak into
a lecture on ethnomusicology or
religion or Middle East studies or video
production and see what you think.

•

581. You need to know to take
archery or golf. Get credit for
learning to correct your slice.

•

582. You need to know that few places
in the world are better to meet people
than your college's swimming pool.

•

583. You need to know to invite your
professor to lunch. Even profs have to eat.

584. You need to know to run
for student office. People will
automatically assume you're smart.

•

585. You need to know that your
school newspaper needs writers.

•

586. You need to know your
school offers free courses on
improving your concentration.

•

587. You need to know there's
an intramural sports team for
the good, the bad, and the ugly.

•

588. You need to know to take a road
trip with the people on your floor. Your
new best friend could be three doors down.

You Need to Know
How to Study

589. You need to know how you learn. Auditory learners process information differently than kinesthetic learners do. Ask your counseling center to help you figure this out.

•

590. You need to know that not everything in your textbook is important. Learn when to skim, when to scan, and when to read.

•

591. You need to know if you're highlighting over 30 percent of a passage, it's time to memorize it.

•

592. You need to know what studying means. It means reading your textbook, reading your notes, rereading everything, and then rereading everything again until you achieve comprehension. This is studying.

593. You need to know studying while drinking beer is not studying. It's drinking. And, while it may be fun, you won't remember anything.

•

594. You need to know if you study at least two hours for every one hour you're in class, your skin will clear up, you'll be infinitely more attractive to the opposite sex, and fame and fortune await.

•

595. You need to know "later" never comes. Don't put studying off till later.

•

596. You need to know that if you got As in high school without studying, you may not have the study habits to succeed in college.

•

597. You need to know math is learned by doing the problems. Over and over again.

598. You need to know to use index cards when reading a book. Write down the page number, note the area of the page, and one or two key words. This will keep you from searching through an entire book to find something.

•

599. You need to know that even if you landed on campus with a full scholarship, you're going to have to work harder than ever before to keep it. Full-scholarship students lose their scholarship money all the time.

•

600. You need to know the study habits you develop as a freshman will either benefit you or haunt you for the next four years.

•

601. You need to know students who overstudy become doctors and lawyers. Life is weird that way.

602. You need to know to drink lots of cold water as you're pulling an all-nighter. This will force you to get up and go to the bathroom often. Even if you're getting drowsy.

•

603. You need to know to close your dorm door when you study. An open door says, "Come on in. Let's party."

•

604. You need to know to study with all the lights on. Especially the later it gets.

•

605. You need to know that studying in bed is a great way to wake up really refreshed for the next morning's test. Doomed, but refreshed.

•

606. You need to know that most students, who don't know what they're talking about, stopped studying too early.

607. You need to know that
many professors post old tests on
the Internet and in the campus library.

•

608. You need to know that if the rest of the class
is four chapters ahead of you, you may want to
cancel this weekend's plans. And next weekend's.

•

609. You need to know how to stay
awake: coffee, washing your face ten times a
night, studying with a friend. More Red Bull.

•

610. You need to know to crank out all your
weekend studying by Friday evening. It's
what the successful students are doing.

•

611. You need to know the A students get ahead
on weekends. It's weird what the brain can do
when it's not sitting in a smoke-filled bar.

612. You need to know that the homework you have your freshman year is just a tune-up for your next three years.

•

613. You need to know to keep a textbook with you at all times. Pull it out while riding the bus, waiting in line, sitting in the doctor's office.

•

614. You need to know failing students have difficulty understanding concepts, terminology, issues, and procedures. If you don't know these, see a tutor.

•

615. You need to know that, in contrast to high school, a college class might only have two or three tests all semester. Blow just one and you're, well, on the five-year plan. Then the six-year plan. Then the I'll-come-back-in-ten-years plan.

616. You need to know that the professors may not review the material you're going to be tested on. You're expected to know it.

•

617. You need to know you're toast if you don't read the assignments, if you're only semi-conscious while reading, or if you expect the professor to teach you everything you need to learn. Burned toast.

•

618. You need to know that, come exam time, you're expected to know everything about each subject. No, it's not fair.

•

619. You need to know there's a difference between reviewing a semester's worth of material and cramming a semester's worth of reading into that same period of time.

620. You need to know the goal of studying is not memorizing but understanding.

621. You need to know CliffsNotes help in understanding things like Shakespeare or Voltaire. But you still have to read the stuff.

622. You need to know the facts about cramming. Studies indicate people appear better able to remember things they have just learned if they are able to sleep soon after (*New York Times*, May 1, 2007).

623. You need to know to call your dad for motivation. You can tell him you don't feel like studying, and he can tell you about living on peanut butter in order to send you to college. You'll feel so guilty you'll stare at the textbooks all night long.

624. You need to know to set goals.
Like doing twenty algebra problems
before calling your girlfriend. Or reading
and understanding an entire chapter before
calling your parents for money. It works.

•

625. You need to know to concentrate
on the text headings as you read a
chapter, not skim over them. Test
questions often come from those headings.

•

626. You need to know your
organizational skills will make
or break you during exam time.

You Need to Know
That If You Have
More Brains and
Drive Than Money,
Community
College Is a Good
Idea . . . Maybe

627. You need to know you can
save a fortune by knocking out your
prerequisites at a community college.

•

628. You need to know that
qualified community-college
students have better odds of being
accepted by the college of their
choice than if they had applied
for admission as a freshman.

•

629. You need to know the other
odds: most kids who start at a
community college never graduate
from a four-year school. It takes
every ounce of discipline you have
to place out of community college.

630. You need to know that
sometimes it's impossible to
transfer community-college
courses to a four-year school.
Check with the four-year
school you're planning to attend.

•

631. You need to know if you're
taking remedial math or English
in a community college, you're like
at least 42 percent of the freshmen
there. And only half of you will pass.

632. You need to know there are
basically two kinds of students
in community college: those who
can't afford four years of a four-year
school and those who barely passed high
school. Guess who goes on to graduate.

•

633. You need to know to not give up
if money is the issue. Organizations
like the Jack Kent Cooke Foundation
help qualified students make the
financial leap from community
college to a four-year school.

You Need to Know How to Tell the Difference Between a Loser Community College and One That Will Propel You to a Four-Year School

634. A good community college:

- Has a focus on liberal arts and science
- Means your classes are filled with people who can add and speak English
- Has programs designed to keep motivated students attending classes together
- Has an honors program
- Offers a curriculum that crosses disciplines
- Has professors who hold advanced degrees
- Features transfer agreements with four-year institutions in-state, guaranteeing you admission and the transfer of core courses if you've kept up your grades
- Has a history of placing students in top four-year institutions
- Can point to community leaders who started there

You Need to Know How to Manage Your Time Since Your Mom Is No Longer Managing It for You

635. You need to know a major
reason bright kids drop out of
college is they fail to manage their time.

•

**636. You need to know that, to a student,
time is more important than money.**

•

637. You need to know to spend four hours
in the library before you spend four hours
clubbing. Students who get the order reversed
spend the spring semester with their mom.

•

**638. You need to know that every day you'll be
making decisions like whether to spend time on
Facebook or get started on writing your paper.**

•

639. You need to know that, on some
large campuses, you can be busy from
7:00 a.m. to midnight and never set foot in
a classroom or open a book. Focus is the key.

640. You need to know a typical night of college homework will look like this:

- Review French vocabulary
- Study seventy pages for International Politics midterm
- Read sixty pages of literature
- Study for humanities midterm
- Research for science project
- Study for science midterm

641. You need to know you could easily wind up in classes that meet at 8:00 a.m., 12:00 noon, and 4:00 p.m. What you do in between those classes will determine whether you go to medical school as a student or an experiment.

642. You need to know that success in college is based on how well you do things you don't want to do when you don't want to do them.

643. You need to know that having
a full schedule isn't the same thing
as accomplishing something that leads
to graduation. Some students have a
full schedule of tanning, partying,
and studying their boyfriends.

•

644. You need to know you'll
feel like you don't have enough time
to study when the truth is you don't
have enough time to party, hold court
in the student center, suntan, play tennis,
nap, play video games, take two hours
for lunch, catch a movie, go to a sorority
meeting, spend two hours on Facebook, and
then study. But you do have time to study.

645. You need to know to invest in a Blackberry or even an old-fashioned pen-and-paper personal day planner. Carry it with you everywhere. Write in it when a professor announces homework or tests. Read tomorrow's plans tonight so you're prepared for...well...tomorrow.

•

646. You need to know there's software that will help you manage your contacts, assignments, lecture notes, and research.

•

647. You need to know that staying organized means you won't have to drive back to the library at 2:00 a.m. to look for class notes—and then tear up your dorm room at 4:00 a.m. because you lost them again.

•

648. You need to know that students who organize their research and lecture notes using database software tend to do better. Curiously, they tend to run companies later in life as well.

649. You need to know that being organized has nothing to do with being neat and clean. It simply means being able to find what you're looking for quickly and accomplishing what you want to accomplish efficiently.

•

650. You need to know that 52 percent of students surveyed felt that partying did not affect their grades. The other 48 percent said partying did affect their grades—and they had a swell time. From what they could remember.

•

651. You need to know how to prioritize what's really important today: researching your term paper; figuring out next semester's schedule; checking out your blonde lab partner's Twitter feed. Okay, what's second most important?

You Need to Know How to Survive the Parties

652. You need to know that, yes,
for the most part, the stories are true.

•

653. You need to know to act like
you've lived without a curfew before.

•

654. You need to know people go to parties to meet
people. Don't sit and drink with the potted plant.

•

655. You need to know that no one has failed to
graduate because of spending too little time partying. In fact, those nerds tend to graduate early.

•

656. You need to know that if you're
going to drink, keep it to one drink an hour—
and have a glass of water or Coke in between.

•

657. You need to know that you can be
arrested for underage possession of alcohol even
if you're just walking down the street with it.
And fines can be as high as $300. Bummer.

658. You need to know if you stay drunk all weekend, you can lose as much as 30 percent of what you learned the previous week. No matter how hard you studied. Pass the milk.

•

659. You need to know your friends won't feel sorry for you when you throw up from partying too much. In fact, they'll take pictures of you and post them on Facebook.

•

660. You need to know to tell yourself there's always going to be another party. There may not, however, be another term paper or semester exam.

•

661. You need to know parties inevitably break out at night. Get your studying done during the day when all is quiet.

•

662. You need to know at least one sober person at a party in case you need help getting home.

663. You need to know you'll have a lot more fun if your homework is done.

•

664. You need to know what the word *moderation* means—and to exercise it.

•

665. You need to know you don't have to get smashed every time you go out. In fact, it makes you look like a goober.

•

666. You need to know if you've had twenty or so drinks at a party, don't go back to your dorm. Go to a hospital.

•

667. You need to know that a study group can take the place of a kegger. Only people bring books, not booze. And as the night goes on, they get smarter, not dumber.

668. You need to know to use partying as a reward for studying. Not a substitution.

•

669. You need to know students fail out of party schools all the time.

•

670. You need to know to not accept a drink from any person you don't know.

•

671. You need to know the person you're leaving the party with.

•

672. You need to know to resist the urge to take off your clothes just because you're on the beach and a camera is pointing at you. Those pictures can be posted on the Internet the next day. And be part of a film by the end of the week.

673. You need to know to bring
enough money for a cab.

•

674. You need to know mixing alcohol with energy
drinks like Red Bull means that, yes, instead of
passing out four hours ago, you can have six more
drinks. This is how college kids wind up in the
hospital injured, raped, or comatose.

•

675. You need to know if you're taking
medication, people will think you've had fifteen
drinks even though you may have only had a sip.

•

676. You need to know life isn't a constant party.
Well, after your freshman year anyway.

You Need to Know More Than You Already Think You Know About Drinking and Drugs

677. You need to know people in college drink
the same or more as when they were in high
school. If you're getting sauced now, save
your tuition money and go straight to rehab.

•

678. You need to know the statement
"I was drunk" isn't an excuse.

•

679. You need to know that studying
for a chemistry final is a lot more
fun than going through detox.

•

680. You need to know you're not better than the
kids who do drugs because all you do is get drunk.
Your brain is leaking the same fluid as theirs.

•

681. You need to know that if
drinking makes you want to fight,
you need to learn two words: club soda.

682. You need to know the odds: up to 20 percent of the students on some campuses have been injured while drinking.

•

683. You need to know there's no safe place at school to get knee-walking drunk. You can fall down your dorm stairs, you can fall out of your bunk, you can fall off your balcony, and you can pass out and collapse in the shower.

•

684. You need to know drunken crowds are dangerous. Whether you're drunk or not.

•

685. You need to know that the applications for many graduate programs ask if you've ever been convicted of a crime . . . like, oh, a DWI.

686. You need to know once you start missing English literature because of your drinking, your days are numbered. Cheers.

•

687. You need to know that if you find yourself having to lie about your drinking, then you need to look at the truth.

•

688. You need to know that if you wake up in the morning without any clothes on and don't remember taking them off, you have a drinking problem.

•

689. You need to know if you wake up in the morning next to someone you don't know, you have a drinking problem.

690. You need to know if you
wake up in the morning with a strange
tattoo, you have a drinking problem.

•

691. You need to know if you need
just one little drink to make it through
class, you have a drinking problem.

•

692. You need to know if you're continually
promising yourself and your boyfriend you're
going to quit, you have a drinking problem.

•

693. You need to know if you're
drinking to escape from the pressures
of college, you have a drinking problem.

•

694. You need to know if you didn't mean
to get drunk, you have a drinking problem.

695. You need to know if you'd rather drink all afternoon than go to class, you have a drinking problem.

•

696. You need to know if your parents cut you off because you've been drinking too much, it's time to seek help.

•

697. You need to know that 40 percent of today's college students report they have engaged in binge drinking. And over 40 percent of college students today don't get their degrees in six years. You're a college student. Connect the dots.

•

698. You need to know that 40 percent of the academic problems students have today are alcohol related.

699. You need to know that 29 percent of college dropouts drop out due to alcohol.

•

700. You need to know that 50 percent of violence in relationships involves alcohol.

•

701. You need to know you won't be considered weird if you don't drink. You'd be just like 30 percent of today's college students.

•

702. You need to know alcohol isn't a meal replacement.

•

703. You need to know alcohol isn't a weight loss plan.

•

704. You need to know the difference between passing out (stupid) and blacking out (dangerous).

705. You need to know that learning how to hold your liquor means you've trained your liver to work overtime. Get on the transplant list now.

•

706. You need to know to avoid drinking games. They're fun to watch, though. Especially the screaming, throwing up, clothing removal, and passing out parts.

•

707. You need to know how to make one drink last all night.

•

708. You need to know that if you've forgotten how much you've had to drink, it's time to stop for the night. And call a cab.

•

709. You need to know that alcohol can lead to waking up next to that person in English lit you said was too disgusting to talk to.

710. You need to know to congratulate yourself when you wake up in a hospital after a night of drinking. You could have killed yourself.

•

711. You need to know that if you have to do a line to be normal for class, you're not normal.

•

712. You need to know what your nose is for.

•

713. You need to know it's impossible to complete even a one-page paper if you need a fix.

•

714. You need to know if you're leaving the campus to hang out with drug dealers, odds are you'll soon be making the evening news.

715. You need to know borrowing your roommate's ADD medicine to stay awake for an exam can make your heart race, give you a panic attack, and cause you to freak out during the exam. "I was stoned" isn't an excuse.

•

716. You need to know that if you buy speed to help you diet or study, the fact is you have no idea what's in the pill. But your dealer knows you're an idiot.

•

717. You need to know that a lot of "brilliant" students never graduate from college because they graduated from marijuana to meth and then to speed, crack, and smack. Many now push grocery carts downtown.

You Need to Know About Relationships

**718. You need to know one
key to succeeding in college
is never feeling alone.**

•

719. You need to know there's an
intimacy in just holding hands that a lot of
college students have never experienced.

•

**720. You need to know a person
who holds your hand isn't making
a long-term commitment.**

•

721. You need to know the absolute
worst reason to attend a college is
because your boyfriend or girlfriend
is there. You've decided in advance
to limit the number of people you meet.

722. You need to know the odds are your high-school relationship won't last three months on campus. If God wants you to be together in four or five years, it doesn't matter if one of you goes to the moon. You'll be back together.

•

723. You need to know that everything changes over time. Including people. And relationships.

•

724. You need to know destructive relationships can wreak havoc on grades, friendships, and bank accounts.

•

725. You need to know a major reason students drop out of college is a relationship gone south.

726. You need to know a healthy relationship can be good for your grades.

•

727. You need to know gossip spreads fast in a dorm.

•

728. You need to know college isn't about finding love. Say it with me: "College is about job opportunities."

•

729. You need to know senior girls don't talk to freshman boys. Unless your name is Kennedy or Rockefeller— and then you can't get rid of them.

•

730. You need to know senior boys are all over freshman girls. Leaving freshman boys in the lurch.

731. You need to know "no strings attached" is an urban myth. Sex always comes with strings attached.

•

732. You need to know pregnancy and a baby will really interfere with graduating.

•

733. You need to know having a relationship with a crazy person will only make your life harder than it already is.

•

734. You need to know that a person who won't let you hang out with your friends now won't think any better of them in two or three years.

•

735. You need to know you don't have to spend every waking moment with the person of your dreams. Really. Go make other friends.

736. You need to know that if you're worried about another person's drug or alcohol abuse, the bigger issue is why you're attracted to them.

•

737. You need to know that someone who calls you all the time to find out where you are or who you are hanging out with needs therapy. And medication. Change your number.

•

738. You need to know if a person is continually criticizing you or making fun of you and you stay with them, you're in an abusive relationship.

•

739. You need to know to flee if a person starts abusing you sexually, emotionally, or physically. You can't make them act differently.

740. You need to know that when a person starts telling you what to wear and you let him, it's you who needs therapy and counseling.

•

741. You need to know a person who has to be with you all the time is dangerous to be alone with.

•

742. You need to know that a person who is continually blaming you for their problems has problems. Flee.

•

743. You need to know the first time you have to make bail for a person is when you should break up.

•

744. You need to know that jealousy isn't romantic. And it can actually be dangerous.

745. You need to know if you find yourself stalking another student, check in at the mental health center before you get arrested.

•

746. You need to know the last thing you want to do is tattoo the name of your sophomore-year boyfriend on your back. It's a hard thing to explain to your junior-year boyfriend.

•

747. You need to know hookups and casual sex is where things get really crazy in college.

•

748. You need to know to ask yourself whether having casual sex supports your personal values, morals, and goals.

•

749. You need to know casual sex can turn people into emotional basket cases.

750. You need to know when the situation and person "feel right," whether or not you should really trust those feelings.

•

751. You need to know to not trust your feelings and emotions after three drinks.

•

752. You need to know the emotional risks of having sex, especially if your partner doesn't want to commit to a long-term relationship.

•

753. You need to know breaking up after a sexual relationship can result in depression, loneliness, torching your midterms, and having your parents refuse to pay for the following semester.

•

754. You need to know that many of the most exclusive campuses now have abstinence clubs. It seems some of the smartest kids don't think college sex is such a good idea.

755. You need to know condoms guard against pregnancy and STDs. If you're sexually active, don't leave home without one.

•

756. You need to know your partner's history of STDs.

•

757. You need to know a rash on your partner isn't good news.

•

758. You need to know that—once again— "I was drunk" isn't an excuse.

•

759. You need to know any sexual conduct— even just lying on top of each other naked and heavily petting—can result in STDs.

•

760. You need to know the results of your partner's HIV test. Make him show you.

761. You need to know your partner.
A simple thing really, but often forgotten
in the heat of the moment.

•

762. You need to know that if
you're feeling pressure to have sex,
it's time to get dressed and go visit
the mental health counselor.

•

763. You need to know that if you
can't comfortably talk about sex with
your partner, you're not ready for it.

•

764. You need to know anyone who
texts you at 2:00 a.m. looking for a
hookup isn't worth texting back.

765. You need to know that if
your partner comes from an abusive
background, you need to leave. Today.

•

766. You need to know alcohol will
only make an abusive relationship worse.

•

767. You need to know college
students who normally carry protection
forget to use it when they're drunk.

•

768. You need to know your friends
aren't having more sex than you.
Especially the disease-free ones.

•

769. You need to know that "No" is a
complete sentence. After that, it's rape.

You Need to Know It's Time to Think Like an Adult

770. You need to know the anxiety, the depression, and the anger you feel the first two or three weeks at college has a name: homesickness.

•

771. You need to know it's normal to miss Mom's cooking and to not want to be responsible for anything. It's also normal to like, you know, get over it.

•

772. You need to know that in college you will acquire behaviors that will last into adulthood. And this includes drinking, thinking, organization, responsibility, how you treat the opposite sex—everything.

•

773. You need to know that if you didn't learn how to do laundry before you left home, you're going to risk total humiliation when everything you own turns pink.

774. You need to know your underwear size. The day may come when you have to buy your own.

•

775. You need to know just because you *can* do something doesn't mean you *should*.

•

776. You need to know that, starting now, you'll be faced with choosing between integrity and security. Like do you write your own essay or pay someone really smart to write it?

•

777. You need to know that if you're "above average," you can shave a year off college by taking between eighteen and twenty-one units a semester. This means less partying, but you could start making money that much sooner.

•

778. You need to know the best cure for worrying in bed is getting up and studying.

779. You need to know why you failed a test. And make the necessary changes to pass the next one.

•

780. You need to know excitement, lack of sleep, bad eating habits, poor study skills—basically, undisciplined freedom—can result in failing grades.

•

781. You need to know that blowing a course or two isn't the end of the world. People have recovered from a bad semester and gone on to medical school.

•

782. You need to know an F paper means you need to work harder. Not hide in your dorm room.

•

783. You need to know to find a mentor.

784. You need to know that even though high school was easy for your brain, you have to study now. Only you may have to learn how to study.

•

785. You need to know to not go around thinking your professors hate you if you're failing.

•

786. You need to know to not take pictures of your body parts with your camera phone and then send them out to your address book. This usually results in total humiliation.

•

787. You need to know a typical week at college includes being embarrassed, depressed, flattered, frustrated, excited, and worried. Not to mention falling in love, fruitlessly, at least once.

788. You need to know being placed on academic probation or academic suspension means you've done just about everything in college except the one thing you're supposed to do.

•

789. You need to know there are few things more humiliating than asking a professor for a letter of recommendation and having him say that he doesn't know who you are.

•

790. You need to know a refrigerator was made to hold something besides beer. Amazingly enough, vegetables, fruit, yogurt, and milk all fit in one.

•

791. You need to know if your friends are leaving joints around your dorm room and continually pulling you away from your studies, you need new friends.

792. You need to know that knowing too few people causes just as many problems as having too much fun.

•

793. You need to know to not blame your loneliness on the fact everyone else is a snob. You're a goober who won't join any clubs, has a bad attitude, and is acting like, well, a snob.

•

794. You need to know to not believe everything you read posted on Internet student message boards. In fact, don't believe *anything* you read there.

•

795. You need to know different people flower at different times. It could happen to you during your sophomore year. Or when you're forty.

796. You need to know a lot of problems get better after you've had a good night's sleep.

•

797. You need to know that if your family has been through a divorce, a death, or a remarriage, you're going to have to work that much harder to cope with stress in college.

•

798. You need to know that if you're feeling like everyone is talking about you, you've seriously underestimated other college students' tendency to think only about themselves.

•

799. You need to know that alcohol doesn't eliminate the stress of being alone. Though after enough drinks, you might find yourself utterly fascinating.

800. You need to know that developing
the ability to cope with adversity is
a rite of passage into adulthood.

•

801. You need to know the solution to
having a difficult time is rarely dropping out
of school. But it may be dropping a difficult
course. And picking it up in the summer.

•

802. You need to know that if you just up and
quit during the first semester, your immaturity
has effectively cost your parents at least $12,000.
If you quit after two years, it's closer to $50,000.

•

803. You need to know that if you need your
parents to run interference for you in college,
your tuition is probably a waste of money.

804. You need to know that one day you'll
be twenty-two. If you work hard enough,
you can be a twenty-two-year-old college
graduate. Or else you could be a
twenty-two-year-old dropout.

•

805. You need to know if you haven't
been to class in two years, it's time
to break the news to your family.

•

806. You need to know you don't need your
parents during registration. Remember
how much you wanted them to leave
you alone in high school? You'll make
mistakes, you'll learn, you'll figure it out.

•

807. You need to know to memorize your Social
Security number. You'll be asked for it a lot.

808. You need to know someone has
to clean the dorm, change the sheets,
and pay the bills. And Mom's at home.

•

809. You need to know college is a good
time to learn to get along with others.

•

810. You need to know a life spent in the
pursuit of happiness results in anything but.

•

811. You need to know God doesn't hate
you just because you're not able to live the
lifestyle you were used to in high school.

•

812. You need to know the world
sees an adult when it sees you.

813. You need to know winning isn't the only thing in life. People who think that start cutting corners early.

•

814. You need to know to accept Gandhi's challenge: "Be the change that you want to see in the world." Start by resisting the urge to cheat just because other students are cheating.

•

815. You need to know to act on your dreams now. Some of the country's most successful entrepreneurs started their companies while in college.

•

816. You need to know to pay your bills on time when you move into an apartment— or you'll learn what cutoff notices look like.

817. You need to know that vacationing in Cabo instead of working as a summer intern will come back to haunt you when all the graduates who interned have jobs and you have a deep, dark tan.

•

818. You need to know how to delay gratification. What would happen if, instead of partying tonight, you studied and then passed your organic chem test, got into dental school, and became so rich you could charter a jet to France? Hmmm. . . .

•

819. You need to know a high IQ doesn't determine wealth. Education, ambition, hard work, and grace play huge roles. People with average IQs get rich all the time.

820. You need to know many career and graduate school plans have been derailed by pictures of drunken, half-naked students being posted on Facebook and Twitter. Employers and graduate school admissions officers have computer access too.

•

821. You need to know many employers view your GPA as the best indicator of work success.

•

822. You need to know many companies don't want to interview anyone with less than a 3.0 grade point average.

823. You need to know working your way through college isn't fun—especially when you're burning your hands in some fast-food kitchen while other students are partying their drunken heads off. But you're prioritizing, showing responsibility, and practicing good decision making—all transferable job skills. And what could possibly show up on the Internet?

•

824. You need to know to not spend time worrying about whether or not you're at the right college when you have semester exams to deal with.

•

825. You need to know you're not a smarter, wiser, or infinitely more capable human being than your parents. Otherwise you wouldn't be calling home for money.

826. You need to know when you're failing—
and get some help. Don't lie to yourself
until the end of the semester.

•

827. You need to know that if you quit school,
the odds are you won't go back at all. And the
longer you're out, the worse the odds become.

•

828. You need to know seemingly
trivial decisions like dropping a course
or working more hours can impact
your college graduation timetable.

•

829. You need to know it's time to stop
talking about how miserable you are.

•

830. You need to know it's smarter
to change your major now than to one day
find yourself stuck in a career you hate.

831. You need to know you control the issues that determine your success.

•

832. You need to know how to write a cover letter. Especially after four years of college.

•

833. You need to know that if you think no one likes you, what you really need is a friend.

•

834. You need to know you'll probably grow apart from some of your close high-school friends. Especially the ones who continue to act like they're in high school.

•

835. You need to know that, by your senior year in college, you'll be rattled by the thought that in a few months you'll be out of school and on your own. Yes, it's scary. Just ask your parents.

836. You need to know how to develop a killer résumé while in college. It goes nicely with a degree.

•

837. You need to know the Top 10 Qualities Employers Seek In Job Candidates (or Things You Should Have Learned in Four Years.)

1. Communication Skills
2. Motivation/Initiative
3. Teamwork
4. Leadership
5. Academic Achievement/GPA
6. Interpersonal Skills
7. Flexibility/Adaptability
8. Technical Skills
9. Honesty and Integrity
10. Analytical/Problem-Solving Skills

You Need to Know
How to Take Care
of Yourself

838. You need to know to shower. Seriously.

•

839. You need to know college is not the place
to starve yourself. Your mind needs nutrition.

•

840. You need to know you're feeding your mind
whether you're eating grilled fish or fried Oreos.

•

841. You need to know to not treat
beer as a major food group.

•

842. You need to know to not eat yourself
into oblivion. Studies show that really over-
weight kids face discrimination from other
kids, teachers, and even their own parents.

•

843. You need to know that a meal ticket
means yes, you can eat as much and as
often as you want to. No, you don't want to.

844. You need to know to not poison yourself. You're an adult. You know what stuff will kill your brain cells.

•

845. You need to know that the vegetarian route means nothing if you're substituting doughnuts and Twinkies for red meat.

•

846. You need to know that, between the beer, pizza, late-night snacks, and make-your-own-dessert stations in the campus cafeteria, you could easily enter your second year fifteen pounds heavier than when you entered your first.

•

847. You need to know vitamins don't substitute for food. You learned this in high school.

848. You need to know skipping breakfast won't make you thinner. Just hungrier. And less able to concentrate.

•

849. You need to know drinking alcohol causes you to eat more. Hence the term *fat drunk*.

•

850. You need to know to eat three nutritional meals a day of rational portions. Four if you're staying up late studying.

•

851. You need to know that not everything on a salad bar is healthy.

•

852. You need to know you're not hungry just because your boyfriend broke up with you. You're emotionally distraught.

853. You need to know to exercise instead of eating when you feel pressure. It's weird, but you'll feel better and you won't gain weight.

•

854. You need to know throwing up before a date means it's time to go visit the mental health center.

•

855. You need to know smoking is forbidden on most campuses. Besides, all it does is make you cough—and stink.

•

856. You need to know that if you see small black things crawling around your dorm floor, it's time to vacuum. Or talk to a counselor.

857. You need to know that the
pounding between your eyes whenever
you think of microbiology is called a migraine.
Your campus health center can help.
So can studying enough to not worry.

•

858. You need to know sleeping helps
your brain unconsciously process the
information you learned and make connections
that lead to new insights. This doesn't happen
trolling through Facebook all night. This
doesn't happen sleeping in class either.

•

859. You need to know to not call
home every time you sneeze, cough,
wheeze, or run a fever. Call the infirmary.
Every college has one. And it's cheap.

860. You need to know to stay on
your parents' health insurance plan—
you may or may not have to stay in school.

•

861. You need to know if you don't
have health insurance then buy your own
through the college. Accidents happen.
Really nasty, expensive accidents.

•

862. You need to know that if you
wash your hands regularly, you can
safely hang with your germ-infested
friends without catching the plague.

•

863. You need to know that runny noses,
chills, fevers, headaches, and nausea generally
mean you have exams in two days and
you're only on chapter 2 of the English lit
text when you should be through chapter 15.

864. You need to know it's easy to go off the deep end. One-third of college students who die every year are freshmen. Suicide, falling off balconies, auto accidents, and alcoholic poisoning lead the list (*USA Today,* 1/25/2006).

865. You need to know your brain can perform only so long on PowerBars and Pop-Tarts before it loses the ability to produce a coherent sentence.

866. You need to know personal hygiene isn't something you can practice every three days or so and stay healthy. Or keep friends.

867. You need to know that one of the best reasons for staying in school is that some of the best hospitals in the nation are housed on college campuses.

You Need to Know
If You've Become
Mental

868. You need to know that if you're trying to decide between taking a test you haven't studied for or taking a handful of pills, it's time to call a counselor. Your college has one.

•

869. You need to know the alternative to staying positive and upbeat is prolonged depression, suicidal thinking, and being asked to take a voluntary leave of absence.

•

870. You need to know the campus psychiatrist is there for students feeling really anxious, alone, or depressed. Don't worry what people think. On some campuses, seeing a shrink is a mark of status.

871. You need to know that if you start hearing voices that aren't your friends' or your parents', it's time to visit the counselor.

•

872. You need to know that suicide is the second leading cause of death for college students.

•

873. You need to know what gets the attention of mental health experts:

- You've been feeling sad, irritable, or depressed for most of every day for weeks, if not months.
- Activities or people you used to enjoy don't seem interesting anymore.
- You can't seem to get anything done. Like that English paper due five weeks ago.
- You've stop attending class and feel tired all the time.

- You have increased or decreased appetite, or you've lost or gained weight.
- You have terminal insomnia.
- You've been unable to get out of bed for two weeks. Because.
- You're calling your professors every night because you're worried or confused.
- You're spending your nights hitting the porn sites or shopping eBay instead of studying in the library.
- You have difficulty concentrating or making decisions. Like whether you should get out of bed—and if you get out of bed, whether you should take off your pajamas.
- You're yelling at your parents even though they are the source of all your money.
- Your friends say you're weird now.
- You seem to want to slug more people than usual.

- You're calling your parents from jail.
- You don't remember going to your econ class because you were drunk when you showed up.
- You cry a lot, no matter where you are. Like in Biology 101. You feel bad for the frogs.
- You feel hopeless and helpless, as if you're stuck in a dark hole and can't get out.
- People like . . . umm . . . your parents or professors comment that you no longer seem to care about your responsibilities or your appearance.
- You think about death a lot.
- You've made a suicide plan.
- Speed makes you feel normal.
- Your creative writing teacher won't be alone in the same room with you.
- You're bingeing or starving yourself.
- Your boyfriend has filed a restraining order.

874. You need to know that you're not alone. Eighty percent of college campuses today have noted a significant increase in serious psychological problems, including severe stress, depression, anxiety, and panic attacks.

•

875. You need to know if you're going nuts, it may be time for medication. Even if you think people who take antidepressants are goobers.

•

876. You need to know you can't just pull yourself out of clinical depression. You can't study yourself out of it. Or eat your way out of it. Or drink your way out of it. You have to deal with it.

877. You need to know medication won't make you instantly better. Neither will it change your personality. But it can help you graduate. And get a job.

•

878. You need to know that if you mix medication with alcohol, you could easily wind up in a hospital or jail.

•

879. You need to know that the best site for learning about antidepressants is www.crazymeds.org. It's profane, hilarious, and written by people who've actually taken the stuff.

880. You need to know medication can help with symptoms, but not events or circumstances. That is where you need counseling.

•

881. You need to know if you get weird, you'll be asked to take a voluntary leave. This is not the end of the world. This is a chance to get your act together.

You Need to Know How to Keep Money Problems From Causing You to Drop Out

882. You need to know the costs of college. According to the College Board, community colleges charge an average annual tuition of $3,347, compared to $9,139 at state universities (for in-state students) and $31,231 at private institutions.

•

883. You need to know the total cost of a four-year school ranges between $100,000 and $200,000. This is why your dad and mom always seem to be in a bad mood.

•

884. You need to know to avoid schools that are too expensive for your budget. Worrying about paying tuition can cause you to study less and work more. Or completely finish off your parents.

885. You need to know to start paying attention to what the university trustees do. Their job is to raise tuition and fees. They do this regularly.

•

886. You need to know that if you work more than twenty hours a week, you're at a higher risk of dropping out.

•

887. You need to know that, while living at home during college isn't cool, living at home when you're thirty because you've racked up $100,000 in student loans is even less cool.

888. You need to know to not use lack of money as an excuse for leaving school. Money is available to people who will do the work.

•

889. You need to know when all the different college fees are due. Don't get thrown out because you're disorganized.

•

890. You need to know to create and live by a budget. You need to know why you're always overdrawn.

•

891. You need to know you can still have a fun social life on a small budget.

892. You need to know about
guaranteed tuition plans that allow
students to pay the same tuition every
year no matter how high the rates rise.

·

893. You need to know that
borrowing money to go to college is
the very best financial decision you
can make at this age. If you graduate.

·

894. You need to know that
if you borrow money to attend
college, you're more likely to stay.

·

895. You need to know every school
has a list of recommended college
lenders that tend to offer students
the path of least resistance.

896. You need to know that
some of those lenders might have
paid off someone at your college in
order to be on that list. You might find a
better deal if you shop around on your own.

●

897. You need to know to
check with your financial aid
officer every year to see if you
can turn your loan into a grant.

●

898. You need to know buying
textbooks at your college bookstore
can cost between $700 and $1000. But you
can save a fortune with just a little effort.

899. You need to know to start at www.bookfinder.com or www.andybrain.com/archive/ textbooks-online.htm.

•

900. You need to know that waiting until classes start to buy your books won't give you time to shop for the best deals. Many colleges and professors list the required textbooks on their Web site.

•

901. You need to know that many expensive textbooks have a paperback equivalent costing up to 90 percent less than the hardcover edition. Check with your professor and then head to the Web.

902. You need to know one
great thing about used books is, not
only are they cheaper, but someone
has already highlighted the text and
made notes in the margins. A sweet deal
unless the previous owner spent the entire
semester highlighting the wrong things.

•

903. You need to know to use your
student loan money to actually finance
your education. Not a spiffy new BMW.

•

904. You need to know how kids have
done it before you: part-time jobs, campus
jobs, selling blood. (Gross, but nice pay.)

905. You need to know your parents are not too rich for you to receive financial aid. Even wealthy families get tuition breaks. It's all about negotiation.

•

906. You need to know to fill out the FAFSA even if your parents are heart surgeons. All money starts here.

•

907. You need to know college tuition aid also comes in the form of loans. With really favorable interest rates. And they're available regardless of need.

•

908. You need to know to live within your means, as meager as they are.

909. You need to know to not trade in
the paid-for car your parents gave you for a
new leased one. Then you'd have car payments.

•

910. You need to know that campus jobs
pay less, but give you greater scheduling
flexibility. That, plus low transportation
expenses, makes it a pretty good trade.

•

911. You need to know that
if you can fax, file, or check
IDs, you can work on campus.

•

912. You need to know that
landing a campus job is now as
competitive as getting into college.

913. You need to know that one of the best things about a campus job is you wind up sitting on your butt most of the day. In other words, they'll pay you to study. Sweet.

●

914. You need to know more than two-thirds of the nation's college students leave with student debt. Whether they have a degree or not.

●

915. You need to know you have to start paying back the loan the day you leave school. (One in five borrowers leaves college without a degree. They report that life sucks.)

916. You need to know that
if you become a teacher,
thousands of dollars in college debt can be
forgiven. Check out
https://studentaid.ed.gov/repay-loans for info.

•

917. You need to know that federal law
requires every student who takes out a federally
insured government loan to attend an exit
interview before graduating. This is where
they tell you, you have to pay everything back.

•

918. You need to know some schools
and lenders may try to take advantage
of you in an exit interview. They'll be
pitching a consolidation loan that combines
all of your student loans into one big loan
with one monthly payment. Talk to your
lawyer or banker before signing anything.

919. You need to know to not
let a debilitating injury to you or
your parents derail your college plans.
Visit your financial aid office and explain
what happened. Things can be worked out.

•

920. You need to know your
primary mission in college is to
graduate. Don't let work, or trying to
keep up with the girl next door, interfere.

•

921. You need to know homework is much
easier to finish if you don't have to work
two jobs to meet credit card payments.

•

922. You need to know how to evaluate credit
card offers with all their different interest rates
and annual fees. This is a seventh-grade math
skill that many college freshmen don't have.

923. You need to know credit card debt
is a major reason kids drop out of college.

•

924. You need to know, since
you're the legal age to sign up for a
credit card, you're also the legal
age to be sued for nonpayment.

•

925. You need to know that credit card
companies charge students a whopping
24 percent interest compared to 14 percent
for most other adults. This is called
getting . . . well, you know what it's called.

•

926. You need to know that
having credit cards is why students
are forced to drop out of school
with $50,000 in credit card debt.

927. You need to know a credit
card doesn't make you independent.
Money makes you independent.

•

928. You need to know your friends
aren't cooler than you just because
they have credit cards. They simply
have the ability to rack up debt faster.

•

929. You need to know a manageable
$30-a-month credit card payment
can skyrocket up to $300 a month
if you are late on one payment and
if you go over your credit limit.

•

930. You need to know credit card late fees
run between three and four times higher
for college students than for working adults.

931. You need to know outstanding credit
card debt can cost you housing, graduate
school admission, your car, a job, maybe
even your ability to secure school loans.

·

932. You need to know to tuck away
some money for emergencies, or you'll still
be paying for them in your late twenties.

·

933. You need to know to not lend
your car. An unfortunate wreck,
cancelled insurance, and lawsuits
can end the brightest college career.

·

934. You need to know to maintain
solid financial status. Overdraft charges and
fees for bounced checks or late payments
can reduce you to living on bean dip.

935. You need to know that one of the best ways to afford college housing is to become an RA in a dorm. It means free housing and sometimes extra money.

•

936. You need to know two words: ramen noodles. They're dirt cheap, and with a little water, they almost become food. College students and mice have been known to live on them for years.

•

937. You need to know to not sell your textbooks in the middle of the semester for date money.

•

938. You need to know you don't have to leave your dorm to earn money. Many kids are now doing virtual internships from their dorm.

939. You need to know that eating
every meal out gets expensive.
Make a sandwich. Save ten dollars.

•

940. You need to know to avoid cash-
advance stores. Interest begins accruing the
day you walk in. And the Mob charges less.

•

941. You need to know that when you live on
campus, you don't have utility bills. If you live
off campus, utility bills are those things you've
been throwing away thinking they're junk mail.

•

942. You need to know you can sell
your blood only a few times a year.

•

943. You need to know to start clipping coupons
if you're living in an apartment. Especially on
Sunday. They can slash your grocery bill.

You Need to Know to Not Leave Your Faith at Home

944. You need to know to let go of your preconceptions about how things will work out. God has a plan too.

•

945. You need to know college will force you to examine your beliefs and values.

•

946. You need to know it's possible to graduate summa cum laude and be accepted into a prestigious medical school and still not find meaning in life.

•

947. You need to know to not set up an intellectual barrier between you and God.

•

948. You need to know the more you learn about cell structure, chemical reactions, and human anatomy, the more you'll experience true wonder at God's creation.

949. You need to know to attend worship services. Even after partying all night before. Research published in the *New York Times* reveals college students who attend religious services regularly do better than those who don't.

•

950. You need to know that kids who go to worship services work harder and are more involved in campus life.

•

951. You need to know to not wait until you're sitting in your semester exam looking at an impossible algebra problem to start up a relationship with God. He could be busy with the student two desks behind you who's been relating to Him all year.

•

952. You need to know the world in which you are about to enter is full of religion.

953. You need to know that striving to lead a good life will help you find happiness.

•

954. You need to know the name of the first book of the Bible. And the last. Most people who leave college can't name either.

•

955. You need to know to volunteer a couple of hours a week. At a homeless shelter or a soup kitchen. It will take your mind off you.

•

956. You need to know Joan of Arc was never married to Noah. This confuses some students.

•

957. You need to know to be open to a real encounter with God.

•

958. You need to know it takes spiritual strength to face adversity. Going to church on a regular basis helps.

959. You need to know you're not alone in your beliefs. Religious activities are offered on campuses more now than in the last century.

•

960. You need to know it's often possible to live in a dorm where matters of faith are part of the daily conversation and routine. Sure beats talking about Katy and Taylor all day.

•

961. You need to know to take your eyes off yourself and ponder how the majority of the world lives on $2 a day. The more you ask how you can help, the less you'll dwell on your own problems. You may even decide you don't have any real problems.

•

962. You need to know the value of spending a summer working on a relief mission to Africa or Mexico.

963. You need to know your
religion course will probably be taught
by an atheist. No, it doesn't make sense.

•

964. You need to know that,
by your sophomore year, you might
find yourself questioning God.
Don't worry. He can handle it.

•

965. You need to know even
prayer can't overcome the
consequences of not studying.

•

966. You need to know to pursue
more than a degree. Pursue a purpose.

•

967. You need to know God's purpose
for you is the reason you're alive.

You Need to Know
How to Handle
Your Parents

968. You need to know the real
reason your parents are calling during the
day is to see if you're going to class. They'll
be calling at night to see if you're studying.

•

969. You need to know your parents
will eventually get over your leaving home.
So if your mother cries whenever you call,
be patient with her.

•

970. You need to know they're destroying their
401(k)s to send you to school. If you come home
whining about how hard college is and how bad
you need a vacation, they will just look at you
and turn the sound up on *Law and Order.*

•

971. You need to know you still
need your parents' advice and
support. Don't leave home without it.

972. You need to know to send
them a letter every now and then.
With a stamp. And not asking for money.

•

973. You need to know that after
two months of college, you will think
that you know everything while your
folks doubt you have the brain cells to find
the garage. This is how tension between
college students and their parents originates.

•

974. You need to know your parents are
making sacrifices so you can go to college.
Don't be flippant about the money.

•

975. You need to know that if Mom and
Dad are paying for college, they will
continually bug you about your grades.

976. You need to know they won't
send you money every time you call.

•

977. You need to know you might
actually have better conversations with your
parents now that you don't see them every day.

•

978. You need to know to show
your parents your report card. If you're
afraid to, use that as a wake-up call.

•

979. You need to know your professors
really don't want to talk to your mom.
Ever. Except maybe at your graduation.

•

980. You need to know that while it's your
parents' money, it's your life. You have to decide
what field interests you, what school you want
to attend, or if you want to take a semester off.

981. You need to know your parents
will think you've come home to see
them and will be baffled as to why you
show up with three months' worth of
dirty laundry and want to hang out with
your loser friends from high school.

•

982. You need to know to not show your
parents the spiffy new tattoo on your butt
right before the Thanksgiving turkey is carved.

•

983. You need to know Dad might encourage
you to do what you love—and then look
stricken when you tell him you've applied
for a nonprofit missionary job in Africa.

•

984. You need to know your
parents will ask if you should do your
homework rather than go out "again."

985. You need to know Mom and Dad won't understand your need to relax in Cabo over the holidays. They think college is relaxing.

•

986. You need to know you can still go on a trip with your parents even though you're in college. It just might do all of you good.

•

987. You need to know that if you call your parents with a problem, their natural reaction isn't to just listen, but to tell you how to solve it. They can't help it.

•

988. You need to know your parents will probably turn your bedroom into a high-end spa including a sauna shower and whirlpool tub with a flat screen TV and Bose surround sound speakers. Don't have a meltdown. It's not a hint. Well, it is a hint.

You Need to Know
What It Takes
to Graduate

·

989. You need to know that
if you treat school like a full-time job,
giving it forty to fifty hours of your
time each week, you'll graduate.

·

**990. You need to know if you
stay mentally and emotionally
healthy, you'll graduate.**

·

991. You need to know if you
hold your spending down so you
don't have to spend more time at
a job while in school, you'll graduate.

992. You need to know if you don't get into an emotionally sick relationship, you'll graduate.

•

993. You need to know if you talk to your professors outside of class, you'll graduate.

•

994. You need to know that if you stay organized, you'll graduate.

•

995. You need to know that if you have a solid spiritual life, you'll graduate.

996. You need to know that if
you're not thinking about killing
yourself every day, you'll graduate.

•

997. You need to know that
if you choose to be happy, resilient,
thoughtful, generous, and
compassionate, you'll graduate.

•

998. You need to know if you
don't make a baby, you'll graduate.

999. You need to know that
if you do the work when it needs
to be done, not when you
feel like doing it, you'll graduate.

•

**1000. You need to know
that if you can find the balance
between studying and fun,
you'll graduate.**

•

1001. You need to know that
if you keep remembering
why you're doing all of this,
you'll graduate.

OTHER BOOKS IN THE
1001 THINGS SERIES BY HARRY HARRISON...

Check out www.raisingparents.com.